Sue Wong
12-8-97
monday

Irish FOOD & FOLKLORE

Irish FOOD & FOLKLORE

Clare Connery

LAUREL
GLEN

First published in the United States by
Laurel Glen Publishing
5880 Oberlin Avenue, Suite 400
San Diego, CA 92121-9653
1-800-284-3580

NOTES
Eggs should be large (sizes 2 and 3) unless otherwise stated. Small eggs are sizes 6 and 7, medium eggs are sizes 4 and 5 and very large eggs are sizes 0 and 1.

Whole milk should be used unless otherwise stated.

Pepper should be freshly ground unless otherwise stated.

Fresh herbs should be used unless otherwise stated. If unavailable, use dried herbs as an alternative and halve the given quantities.

Ovens should be preheated to the specified temperature— if using a convection oven, follow the manufacturer's instructions for adjusting the time and temperature.

Publishing Director: Laura Bamford
Commissioning Editor: Nicola Hill
Senior Editor: Sasha Judelson
Assistant Editor: Catharine Davey
Art Director: Keith Martin
Senior Designer: Louise Leffler
Designer: Les Needham
Picture Researcher: Claire Gouldstone
Production Controller: Melanie Frantz

Acknowledgments

Bill Doyle: back and front flaps, 1, 3, 5, 7, 8, 9, 10, 11, 12, 22, 34, 36, 49, 56, 66, 76, 85, 94, 97, 104, 106, 112, 117, 120, 132, 136, 139
Reed International Books Ltd./Christopher Hill 15, 18, 27, 31, 35, 39, 43, 47, 50, 55, 59, 62, 67, 71, 75, 79, 82, 87, 91, 95, 98, 103, 107, 111, 114, 119, 123, 127, 131, 135, 138
R.S. Magowan: 28, 40, 58, 92
Alan Newnham: Front jacket inset
Caroline Jones: Jacket spine & flaps main pic.

First published in Great Britain in 1996 by Hamlyn, an imprint of
Reed Consumer Books Limited, Michelin House, 81 Fulham Road,
London, SW3 6RB and Auckland, Melbourne, Singapore and Toronto

Copyright © 1997 Reed International Books Limited

ISBN 1-57145-629-5

Library of Congress Cataloging in Publication Data available upon request.

1 2 3 4 5 97 98 99 00 01

Printed and bound in China

Contents

introduction

Ireland is a beguiling and charming land with a culture steeped in myth and legend, fairy tale and folklore. The very breath of the wind in the trees, the babbling of the water in the stream, the lowing of the cattle in the deep green pastures, and the crackling of the fire in the hearth all draw us into Ireland's mysterious past. Its foods, feasts, and festivals are linked to the timeless rural calendar and the changing seasons of the year. Here the past is evoked and the spirits of Ireland, with the bounty from the land, sea, and shore, are laid before you in words and pictures.

Myth and legend, fact and fiction are inextricably intertwined within the psyche of Ireland. Cultural traditions and the folklore of the past are never too far from the surface, and still carry weight, if only in superstition. In what is still largely an agricultural country, the pattern of everyday life is bound to the vagaries of nature, and many of the festivals and rituals are closely associated with the changing seasons.

This is not to say that Ireland is unsophisticated. In every technical sense she is a modern nation. However, in spite of this, there is still a fascination with the past, in particular for a period which spanned a thousand years, from about 500 B.C. During this time, the richness of the Celtic culture, with its highly developed religion and sophisticated law system, was the creative force. Celtic scholarship and knowledge, was, for many centuries, passed on orally, rather than written down. The spoken word was therefore all powerful. The beliefs, codes of behavior, social systems, folklore, myths, legends, poetry, and song, which bound the people together, giving them a sense of continuity and identity, were entrusted to an elite of Druids (philosophers), seers (prophets), and bards (lyric poets), who preserved this unique body of knowledge through the oral tradition. It was not until the seventh century A.D. that the myths and stories of Celtic culture were written down by monastic scribes. Such tales portray a tribal and rural society of gods and goddesses, warrior princes of major and minor kingdoms, battles, cattle raids, feasting, fertility, and heroism.

IRISH MYTH AND LEGEND

Irish mythology is, in essence, heroic. Colossal figures, endowed with magical powers, dominate. The Tuatha de Danaan (the people of the goddess Dana) were the god-like rulers of the pre-Christian Irish, imbued with super-human traits. Dagda was their leader. He possessed two implements with magical powers: a gigantic club, one end of which could slay enemies; the other end which could heal the sick. He also had a huge cauldron, large enough to contain food for a whole tribe, a testament to his own enormous appetite. At the mythical battle of Magh Tuireadh, his enemies filled the cauldron with a gargantuan stew of goat, sheep, swine, meal, and fat. Dagda was forced to eat the stew, using his huge ladle (big enough to hold a man and a woman). He triumphed, consuming the stew with ease. This epic tale covers many of the recurrent themes of Irish mythology and folklore, typically dealing with fertility, plenty, and victory over all enemies, including hunger.

Eventually the Tuatha de Danaan were defeated by invaders and scattered and shrank in both size and importance. This diminishing of stature was reinforced by the early Christian scribes, who were more inclined to accept the elevation to heroic status of mythical, larger-than-life characters rather than gods. As W. B. Yeats stated in *The Book of Fairy and Folk Tales of Ireland*, "the pagan heroes grew bigger and bigger until they turned into giants."

The two most renowned heroes in Irish folklore are Cúchalainn, reputedly the son of the God Lugh, and Fionn MacCumhail (Finn Mac Cool). These are the principal participants of the most famous Irish cycles: the *Ulster* or *Red Branch Cycle* and the *Fenian Cycle*. The former is the greatest of all Irish sagas, and the most famous story in the cycle, that of the Tain Bó Cuailgne ("The Cattle Raid of Cooley") tells how Medb (Maeve), the much married Queen of Connacht, through envy of her husband's possessions, leads an army to capture the famous Brown Bull of Cuailgne. Cúchulainn, the champion warrior of all Ireland, defends Ulster single-handed against Medb's forces. This revered warrior, who does not fear death, is also the central figure in another epic saga, *The Champion's Portion*, also known as *Bricriu's Feast*—where food plays a significant role, the "champion's portion" being the reward for the undisputed champion. At Bricriu's Feast, the champion's portion as described by Frank Delaney in *Legends of the*

Celts contains "a seven year old boar, ripe and sweet, which, since it was born, had been fed only on sweetened porridge, oatmeal, fresh milk, nuts, wheat, meat, and broth, according to the seasons. In addition, he had a cow, seven years old too, who, since birth

had been fed only heather, herbs, corn, and sweet meadow grass. And to accompany this cauldron full of wine, pig meat, and beef, one hundred wheat cakes had been cooked in honey using a bushel of wheat to every four cakes."

Because Cúchulainn's status as champion is questioned by rival warriors, a long series of physical trials is instigated against these pretenders. Meanwhile, the

feasting continues while Cúchulainn establishes his supremacy before returning to claim the "champion's portion".

Almost equal in status to the figure of Cúchulainn is Fionn MacCumhail, the most celebrated leader of the Fianna (The Royal Bodyguard of the High Kings), who, as a young man, was the pupil of Finegas, a Druid poet. Finegas had for many years sought to catch the "Salmon of Knowledge," a red-spotted fish, which acquired its knowledge by eating the berries of the rowan as they fell into the water. When eventually he succeeds, Finegas gives the fish to Fionn to cook, who, in doing so, burns his fingers on the fish and acquires wisdom.

As with Cúchulainn, Fionn has many physical and mystical adventures, including his defeat of Daire Dawn (King of the World). His unrequited love for Grainne and his pursuit of her and Diarmuid, her lover, is a classic love epic.

FAIRIES AND FOLKLORE

The legends and stories of Ireland are not only peopled with heroic warriors and mystical gods but are filled with strange and intriguing tales of "little people," with the power to enchant, befuddle, and outwit humankind. Historical research explains these tales of "little people" as the literal shrinking of the pagan gods of Ireland on the arrival of Christianity. From this time, the gods lost their religious significance, receding into legend and fairy tale, but retaining magical powers in the imagination of the people.

The Irish word for fairy is *sidheóg*, which comes from the description of the old Irish gods who were relegated to fairy status as *aés sídhe*—"the people of the hills." Intimately associated with rural life, they are reputed to be swift to bless and quick to anger, thus symbolizing a combination of good and evil, both harbingers of fortune and misfortune. They must therefore be respected and placated. The tradition of leaving crumbs from the evening meal by the hearth, a saucer of milk on the bedroom windowsill, and glowing embers in the fireplace as a welcome, are the most common examples.

The fairies can be divided into two principal groups: trooping fairies and solitary fairies. The trooping fairies are usually dressed in green and are mostly friendly; blessed with the power of healing, they help people in trouble. The solitary fairies are dressed in red, prefer their own company, and cause mischief. Some of the more important solitary fairies are:

THE LEPRECHAUN (*Leith Bhrogan*) who is in fact the god Lugh, who was driven underground with the other gods and whose image was diminished in popular folklore into a fairy craftsman, a shoemaker, or tailor. He is somewhat ill-tempered and possesses a crock of gold, to be given to whoever catches him.

THE POOKA (*Púca*) is a malevolent fairy, capable of assuming any shape, usually animal, and is particularly troublesome to travelers, who may unwittingly jump on his back when the pooka takes the shape of a horse.

THE BANSHEE (*Bean Sidhé*) is a "woman of the hills" (also known as the "lady of death"), who attaches herself to a family and warns of approaching death by emitting an eerie wailing and crying. The banshee is sometimes seen accompanied by the coach-a-bower, a funeral carriage drawn by a headless horse and driven by the headless Dallahan.

Music has always served as a foundation stone to the

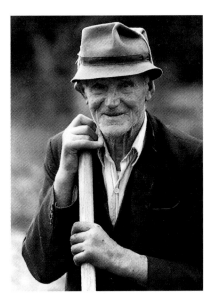

cultural life of Ireland. It therefore seems fitting that fairy music should be a central source for the powers of the "little people." Legend tells of magical music capable of healing the sick and inspiring great men, but also of enticing young children away from the mortal world and into fairyland; a changeling child is left by the fairies in the place of the mortal baby.

Come away! O, human child!
To the woods and waters wild
With a fairy hand in hand,
For the world's more full of
Weeping than you can understand
(W.B. Yeats, "The Stolen Child")

Tir-na-N-og or *Tir-inna-Beo* means "Country of the Young" or "Land of the Living," and is the fairyland of Irish mythology. It is often interpreted as symbolizing the afterlife, a heavenly land that you can only reach by journeying. On this mythical isle, neither death nor old age exist and the inhabitants know neither pain nor sadness.

FEASTS AND FESTIVALS

Mythical folk, whether the larger-than-life characters of heroic legend, or the fairies of the fields, are noted for their appetite for food, and in this respect they are no different from the mortals who toil to produce their sustenance from the countryside.

Four great seasonal pagan Celtic festivals are recorded in mythical tradition, all associated with the farming year—Imbolic (February), Beltaine (May), Lughnasa (August), and Samhain (November). Each of these quarters had its own specific activities and celebrations influenced not only by pastoral and arable traditions, but also by pagan and Christian legend and folklore.

Imbolic

The start of the year in Ireland's rural calendar is the Imbolic festival (February), the beginning of spring. This was linked with the cult of Brigid, daughter of Dagda, a

multifunctional goddess who protected women in childbirth, presided over the ale harvest, and was also associated with milk and butter production, poetry, and property. She retained many of her pagan roles even when she was adopted as a saint by the Christian church.

It was said that on St. Brigid's day, the saint placed her foot in the water and warmed it, giving rise to the belief that from that time on the weather should improve, spring plowing could begin and milk and butter production would increase. On St. Brigid's eve, rushes were fashioned into protective charms known as Brigid's crosses to protect the house and livestock from harm and fire. Milk and butter were particularly susceptible to supernatural influences and, for that reason, the first rich milk given by newly calved cows, called "beastlings," was poured on the roots of fairy thorn trees to appease the "little people." When the butter was made, a small ball of it was smeared or tossed on top of the dresser as an offering to the fairies.

On the coast, the spring tide closest to the festival was believed to be the greatest of the year, and so it became the time when the people gathered seaweed to fertilize their crops and collected shellfish and other produce of the shore. In some parts of the country a limpet or periwinkle was placed at the four corners of the house to bring good luck to the fishermen and draw a bountiful harvest from the sea. There were also celebrations in the house and a special festive supper prepared. Flummery, a type of oatmeal blancmange, and sowans, an oatmeal drink, along with apple cake, apple dumplings, and a fruit bread called barm brac, butter freshly churned that day, and buttermilk, were served. The main dishes ranged from colcannon—mashed potatoes with spring onions and shredded cabbage—to fowl, bacon, and sometimes mutton. It was also customary to give gifts of butter, butter-milk, or pieces of meat to poor neighbors. Indeed, pieces of bread and butter, a cake, or dish of porridge were often left out for St. Brigid herself.

Beltaine

The next major festival in the rural calendar is the Gaelic Beltaine, the feast of the fires of "Bel" (Bilé, the God of life and death). This falls at the beginning of May to celebrate the beginning of summer and triumph over the dark powers. Many superstitions were associated with May Day, particularly those connected with the supernatural world. Witches and fairies were thought to be active and precautions were taken to ward off their evil intentions.

Not only were wells, fields, byres, and houses guarded, but on May eve, bonfires were lit and both men and women leapt over the flames before driving their cattle through smoldering ashes or between two small fires to protect them from evil spells. Milk was poured on the threshold of the house and around fairy thorn trees. May flowers were crushed to provide a juice which was then used to wash the cows' udders. Sometimes the cows' backs were marked with the sign of a cross and, after milking on May Day, a cross was made with the froth from the milk. A bunch of primroses was tied to each cow's tail to protect it against malevolent fairies. A sprig of rowan was also thought to protect against evil and was hung on the byre door, on the milk pail, or on the cow's horns. Sometimes, not even

rowan offered protection against the butter-stealing fairies and, as a result, no milk was given away on May Day and no stranger was allowed to milk the cows. A small quantity of the butter that was made on this day was kept in the dairy for the rest of the season.

Lughnasa

The beginning of harvest was marked by the festival of Lughnasa on August 1, a Druidic festival, held in honor of the god Lugh, to ensure that the corn was safely gathered in. Corn dollies were formed out of the last sheaf to be cut, and it was customary for the first flour ground from the harvest to be made into a loaf of bread and porridge. When the corn was gathered, it was time for the harvest of the hedges and orchards.

Blackberries, whortleberries, blaeberries (billberries), wild raspberries, and strawberries were collected, along with the sacred apples. Finally, nuts were gathered and stored, particularly the hazelnut, which, when grown by a stream, was believed to represent kernels of wisdom. Christianity adapted this feast and named it Lammas (Feast of the First Fruits).

Samhain

Many of these feasts and celebrations pale into insignificance when compared to the festival of Samhain, which marks the dying, or end, of the rural year on All-Hallows Eve, October 31, better known now as Halloween. It was an intensely spiritual time, for it was then that the "other world" became visible to mankind and when spiritual forces were let loose on the human world. On Halloween, it is believed that the spirits and ghosts set out to wreak vengeance on the living. It was thought to be unlucky not to make preparations for the return of the dead, so the door of the house was left open, seats set around the fire, and sowans left ready for the spirits.

The crops should, by now, have all been gathered in. No fruits were picked after this time, for it was thought that the Pooka was busy destroying them by spitting on them. The animals were brought in from their summer pastures; some were slaughtered and some kept for breeding. It was a time for family celebrations, markets, fairs and feasts and there are many foods associated with the occasion.

The vigil of the Feast of All Saints has for many centuries been a day of abstinence, so in general, meat was not eaten. However, there were many other traditional dishes to compensate, using the produce of the harvest—apple cake, potato apple cake, boxty pancakes, bread and dumplings, potato puddings and colcannon, barm brack, oatcakes, batter pancakes and blackberry pies, in addition to apples and nuts—all were favorites of this season.

No matter what the dish chosen, it was thought to bring luck if a wedding ring and other charms were baked inside it. This would decide the destiny for the coming year of the person finding it on his or her plate.

Through all the changing seasons of the year with their associated foods and customs, there is not only a vital relationship between man, his animals, his crops, and the countryside, but also a constant and unbroken link with the past. Although the myths, legends, and fairy stories of Ireland's heroic and mystical past may seem to have small relevance in today's sophisticated society, they still have the power to inspire, entertain, comfort, and sustain. After all, the past lives on in our minds, in our landscape, and the dishes we take to our table.

soups

Soup has always been important in the Irish diet. It was often served at every meal or as the basis of the meal itself, when it was so thick and rich with meat, vegetables, and potatoes, that it was called an "atin and drinkin" soup. Soups were made from whatever ingredients were available: wild herbs, vegetables, seeds, nuts, and grains, along with meat, fish, shellfish, game, and poultry. One of the earliest soups was made from ground oatmeal, boiled in water, with chopped vegetables. When meat was added to it, it was referred to as broth.

Purée of Potato Soup with Bacon & Chives

¼ cup butter

1 large onion, roughly chopped

1½ lbs. potatoes, peeled and roughly chopped

3½ cups chicken stock

3½ cups milk

1¼ cup light cream

6 slices of bacon, chopped and crisply fried

salt and pepper

1 tablespoon snipped chives, to garnish

Melt the butter in a large saucepan and fry the onion until soft, but not brown. Add the potatoes, stock, and milk, and season with salt and pepper. Bring to a boil, then reduce the heat and simmer for 40–45 minutes, stirring occasionally to prevent the potatoes from sticking.

Purée the soup in a blender or food processor until smooth. Return to the pan, taste and adjust the seasoning if necessary and stir in the cream and bacon. Bring to a boil and serve in individual soup bowls garnished with snipped chives.

COOK'S NOTES
Water can be used instead of chicken stock but the result will be much less flavorful. Vegetable stock, even from a bouillon cube, would be preferable.

Serves 6–8
Preparation time: 15–20 minutes
Cooking time: 45–50 minutes

They make the blood warmer,

You'll feel like a farmer,

For this is every cook's opinion,

No savory dish without an onion.

(JONATHAN SWIFT)

Leek & Potato Soup

2 tablespoons butter

2 large leeks, finely sliced

½ lb. potatoes, roughly diced

1 onion, roughly chopped

3½ cups chicken stock or water

1¼ cups milk

salt and pepper

1 tablespoon snipped chives, to garnish

Melt the butter in a large saucepan, add the leeks, potatoes, and onion. Stir well to coat with the butter. Cover tightly with a piece of waxed paper and cook over a very gentle heat for about 15 minutes until softening, stirring frequently to prevent the vegetables from turning brown.

Add the stock or water and milk and season with salt and pepper. Bring to a boil, reduce the heat and simmer gently for about 20 minutes until the vegetables are tender.

Purée the soup in a blender or food processor until smooth, then return to the saucepan, adjust the seasoning if necessary and when very hot, pour into individual bowls. Garnish with chives.

Serves 4–6
Preparation time 15 minutes
Cooking time: 35 minutes

Spinach & Oatmeal Broth

¼ cup butter

1 onion, chopped

2 tablespoons oatmeal

9 oz. spinach

2 oz. potatoes, diced

3½ cups chicken stock

pinch grated nutmeg

1¼ cup milk or cream

salt and pepper

For the garnish:

grated nutmeg

oatmeal

Melt the butter in a large saucepan and fry the onion until soft but not brown. Stir in the oatmeal and continue to cook until the oatmeal is beginning to color slightly.

Wash the spinach, remove any tough stems, and chop the leaves roughly. Add the stock and nutmeg to the pan along with the potatoes, and season with salt and pepper. Bring to a boil and then reduce the heat and simmer gently for 10–20 minutes until the spinach is just cooked.

Purée in a blender and then return to the pan and add the milk or cream. Taste and adjust the seasoning if necessary. Bring to a boil and serve immediately, sprinkled with a little nutmeg and oatmeal.

COOK'S NOTES
Use sorrel instead of spinach or a mixture of both. Cook for the minimum time to retain the color.

Serves 4–6
Preparation time: 5 minutes
Cooking time: 40 minutes

Lentil & Bacon Broth

Rinse the ham shank in cold water, put it into a large saucepan and cover with water. Bring to a boil. This will remove any excess salt from the ham and bring foam to the surface. Pour off this water, rinse the pan and start again with 10 cups fresh cold water. Add the lentils, onions, carrots, and turnip, bring to a boil, reduce the heat and simmer for 1½ hours. Add the potatoes and cook for a further 30 minutes until the meat is tender and the broth rich and thick.

Remove the ham from the broth, peel off the skin and cut the meat into small cubes. Return to the broth, season to taste and stir in the parsley.

Serves 8–10
Preparation time: 15 minutes
Cooking time: 2 hours

1 ham shank from 1–2 lbs. in weight

6 oz. split red lentils, rinsed

2 large onions, finely diced

2 large carrots, finely diced

6 oz. turnip, finely diced

1 lb. potatoes, finely diced

3 tablespoons finely chopped parsley

salt and pepper

Carrot & Herb Soup

Melt the butter in a large saucepan, add the vegetables and garlic and cook gently over low heat until soft but not brown. Add the stock, bouquet garni, and mace. Season with salt and pepper. Bring to a boil and then reduce the heat and simmer gently for 45 minutes–1 hour until the vegetables are tender.

Remove the bouquet garni and purée the soup in a blender or food processor until smooth. Return to the saucepan, add the cream and bring to a boil. Mix the herbs together and stir three quarters of them into the soup. Serve in individual soup bowls garnished with the croutons and remaining herbs.

COOK'S NOTES
To make croutons, remove the crusts from 2 slices of bread and cut each slice into ¼-inch cubes. Fry in a little hot oil until golden-brown on all sides. Drain on paper towels before use.

Serves 6
Preparation time: 10 minutes
Cooking time: 1 hour

2 tablespoons butter

1 large onion, finely sliced

1 lb. carrots, sliced

1 small potato, sliced

1 clove garlic, chopped

4½ cups chicken stock

1 bouquet garni (see Cook's Notes, p. 19)

pinch ground mace

⅔ cup cream

2 tablespoons finely chopped cilantro

1 tablespoon finely chopped parsley

1 tablespoon finely chopped chervil

salt and pepper

croutons, to garnish (see Cook's Notes)

Mushroom Soup with Crispy Bacon

¼ cup butter

1 onion, finely chopped

1 clove garlic, finely chopped

12 oz. mushrooms, thinly sliced

2 tablespoons flour

2½ cups vegetable or chicken stock

⅔ cup milk

1 tablespoon cooking sherry (optional)

⅔ cup light cream

4 slices bacon, cooked until crisp and broken into small pieces

salt and pepper

sprigs of fresh chervil, to garnish

Melt the butter in a large pan and fry the onion, garlic, and mushrooms until soft and beginning to brown. Sprinkle on the flour and stir to combine. Gradually pour in the stock and milk, stirring well to blend. Bring to a boil, then reduce the heat and simmer for approximately 15–20 minutes.

Add salt and pepper to taste, along with the sherry (if using), and half the cream. Reheat, then divide among 4–6 individual soup bowls. Whip the remaining cream until it is just holding its shape, then spoon a little on top of each bowl of soup. Sprinkle with the bacon pieces and garnish with a sprig of fresh chervil.

COOK'S NOTES
A mixture of cultivated and wild mushrooms gives the soup a very special flavor. For a smoother soup, purée before adding the cream.

Serves 4–6
Preparation time: 15 minutes
Cooking time: 20 minutes

Mussel Soup with Saffron & Garlic

Prepare the mussels (see Cook's Notes). Put 2 tablespoons of the butter in a very large saucepan, add one third of the onion and leek and cook until soft. Add the mussels, bouquets garnis, and the white wine. Cover with the saucepan lid and cook on high heat for 4–5 minutes, stirring the mussels from time to time. When all the mussel shells have opened, drain through a strainer lined with cheesecloth placed over a bowl to catch the cooking juices. Remove the mussels from their shells, discarding any which haven't opened. Refrigerate until required.

Gently fry the garlic, carrots, and celery in the remaining butter until soft. Add the fish stock and the reserved mussel juices. Add the mussels, reserving 12 to garnish the soup. Bring to a boil, reduce the heat and cook gently for 20 minutes. Add the saffron, stir in the cream, and blend in a blender or food processor until smooth.

Return to the pan, taste and adjust the seasoning if necessary, stir in the reserved whole mussels and return to a boil. Serve immediately in individual soup bowls garnished with chervil fronds.

COOK'S NOTES

To prepare mussels, wash under cold running water and scrape, removing the "beard" (the hairy attachment protruding from the mussel) and any barnacles attached to the shells. Discard any mussels that are open or damaged.

A bouquet garni is a bunch of fresh herbs generally consisting of parsley stalks, a sprig of thyme, a bay leaf and a blade of mace tied together. This is added to soups and stews to give additional flavor.

Serves 4–6
Preparation time: 30 minutes
Cooking time: 25 minutes

30–40 fresh, live mussels, approximately 3 lbs.

6 tablespoons butter

1 onion, finely sliced

6 oz. leek, white part only, finely sliced

2 bouquets garnis (see Cook's Notes)

½ cup dry white wine

2 cloves garlic, crushed

6 oz. carrot, finely sliced

1 celery stalk, finely sliced

3½ cups fish stock (see page 44)

pinch saffron

⅔ cup heavy cream

salt and pepper

fronds of chervil, to garnish

Game Broth with Potato & Herb Dumplings

6 cups game stock (see Cook's Notes)

1 onion, finely diced

1 carrot, finely diced

1 celery stalk, finely diced

4 oz. turnip, finely diced

1 large potato, finely diced

sprigs of parsley, to garnish

For the dumplings:

1 tablespoon butter

1 tablespoon finely chopped onion

½ lb. potatoes, cooked and mashed

1 tablespoon semolina

2 tablespoons finely chopped parsley

pinch chopped thyme

pinch nutmeg

beaten egg, to bind

about 2 tablespoons flour

salt and pepper

Put the game stock, onion, carrot, celery, turnip and potato into a large saucepan, bring to a boil, then reduce the heat and simmer for 20 minutes until the vegetables are tender.

Meanwhile, prepare the dumplings. Melt the butter in a saucepan and fry the onion until soft but not brown. Stir the softened onion into the potatoes along with the semolina, parsley, thyme, and nutmeg. Season with salt and pepper. Add a little beaten egg and enough flour to make a stiff mixture. Roll teaspoons of this dough into 16 balls using a little flour to keep the mixture from sticking. Drop the dumplings into the hot soup and cook gently for 10 minutes until they float. Divide the dumplings among 8 soup bowls and ladle on the broth. Garnish each bowl with a sprig of parsley and serve immediately.

COOK'S NOTES
This is an excellent way of using leftover bones and trimmings from roast game.

To make the stock, heat a little oil in a pan and brown 1½ lbs. bones, etc. with 1 large carrot, 1 onion, 1 leek, and 1 celery stalk, roughly sliced. Add 5 cups water and a bunch of herbs. Bring to a boil, then simmer gently for at least 2 hours before straining.

Serves 8
Preparation time: 20 minutes
Cooking time: 30 minutes

Farmhouse Broth

Put the meat into a large saucepan with 8 cups water and bring to a boil. Skim the foam from the surface, then add all the remaining ingredients, except the parsley. Reduce the heat and simmer gently for 2–3 hours until the meat is tender and the soup thick.

Lift the meat from the pot, remove from the bone, discard excess fat and cut into thin strips. Return the meat to the soup, taste and adjust the seasoning if necessary, and stir in the parsley.

This soup is traditionally eaten with a freshly boiled, floury potato served in the middle. This makes a very substantial snack or main meal.

Serves 8–10
Preparation time: 20–30 minutes
Cooking time: 2–3 hours

12 oz.–1 lb. beef shank or brisket of beef on the bone

1 oz. split green peas

1 oz. red lentils

1 oz. pearl barley

4 oz. leek, white and green parts, finely chopped

4 oz. carrot, finely chopped

2 oz. turnip, finely chopped

1 onion, finely chopped

1 celery stalk, finely chopped

salt and pepper

2 tablespoons finely chopped parsley, to garnish

Ham & Pea Soup

Melt the butter in a pan and fry the onion, carrot and two thirds of the bacon gently until soft; this will take about 15 minutes. Add the drained split peas, bay leaf, ham bone, and 5 cups water. Bring to a boil, then reduce the heat and simmer gently for 1 hour.

Remove from the heat and discard the ham bone. Season with pepper and salt if necessary. Return the saucepan to the heat. Fry the remaining bacon in a hot pan until crisp, then add to the soup along with 1 tablespoon of the chives. Serve in individual soup bowls and garnish with the remaining chives.

Serves 6
Preparation time: 10 minutes, plus soaking time
Cooking time: 1¼ hours

¼ cup butter

1 large onion, roughly chopped

1 large carrot, roughly chopped

4 thick slices of bacon, approximately 6 oz., diced

8 oz. yellow or green split peas (soaked for 4–6 hours, then drained)

1 small bay leaf

1 ham bone

salt and pepper

2 tablespoons finely chopped chives

appetizers & snacks

The introduction of a first course, other than soup, is a very recent addition to the traditional Irish menu of soup, main course, and dessert. In this section, many of Ireland's best loved products are used to create a tempting overture to the meal. Some of the dishes owe their origins to natural country thrift, where it was considered wrong to waste anything, even the leftovers; hence the black puddings and pâtés. Even in "lean times" some sustenance could be found in the foods gathered from the woods and seashore.

Grilled Goat Cheese on Soda Bread with Bacon & Tomatoes

1 farl of soda bread, split in half (see page 124)

2 slices cut from a cylindrical goat cheese, ½-inch thick

6 cherry tomatoes, halved

1 tablespoon oil

4 slices Canadian bacon, cut into strips

4–5 chives, cut in 1-inch lengths

2 sprigs of chervil or dill, to garnish

Using a pastry cutter slightly larger than the diameter of the goat cheese, cut a circle from each half of the soda farl. Toast the cut side until pale golden in color. Place a circle of cheese on top and put under a preheated hot broiler for 3–4 minutes until the cheese begins to melt and turns golden on top. Heat the cherry tomato halves at the same time.

Meanwhile, heat the oil in a pan and fry the bacon strips until crisp and brown. Drain well on paper towels. Place the pieces of toasted bread and cheese in the center of two serving plates. Arrange the tomatoes and bacon around the toasted cheese and sprinkle with the chives. Garnish with the fresh herb sprigs.

COOK'S NOTES
Irish blue cheese, such as Cashel Blue or Rathgore, makes an excellent alternative to the goat cheese. For a light snack or lunch, serve 2 pieces of the broiled cheese per person with a mixed green salad.

Serves 2
Preparation time: 5 minutes
Cooking time: 5–8 minutes

Did you ever eat a forkful

And dip it in the lake

Of heather flavored butter,

That your mother used to make?

(TRADITIONAL RHYME)

Wild Mushroom Omelet

Melt two thirds of the butter in a small skillet and cook the mushrooms until soft but holding their shape. Keep warm.

Put the eggs and 1 teaspoon cold water into a small bowl, season with salt and pepper, and add the herbs. Beat lightly with a fork to blend. Stir in the mushrooms.

Melt the remaining butter in an 8-inch omelet pan or nonstick skillet and when it foams, pour on the egg mixture. Quickly stir the egg 3–4 times with a fork, then pull the egg from the edges of the pan into the center, tilting the pan so that the liquid egg flows toward the hot surface. When the egg ceases to flow and the omelet looks set but still soft on top, it is cooked.

Using a spatula, fold the edge of the omelet that is closest to the skillet handle toward the center and then the opposite edge on top. Turn the omelet out onto a warm plate seam side down. Garnish with a sprig of parsley and serve immediately.

COOK'S NOTES

The omelet can also be made with cultivated mushrooms or a combination of cultivated and wild mushrooms of whatever varieties are available.

Serves 1
Preparation time: 10 minutes
Cooking time: 5–8 minutes

2 tablespoons butter

2 oz. wild mushrooms, cleaned, trimmed, and sliced

3 eggs

1 teaspoon finely chopped herbs, such as parsley, chives, and chervil

salt and pepper

sprig of flat leaf parsley, to garnish

Cockles & Mussels with Bacon

50 fresh, live mussels, approximately 6 lbs., washed, scrubbed, barnacles and beard removed (see Cook's Notes, page 19)

30 cockles, approximately 12 oz., washed and scrubbed

8 slices bacon

¼ cup butter

1 onion, finely chopped

2 tablespoons finely chopped parsley

1 teaspoon finely chopped chives

salt and pepper

4 sprigs of watercress, to garnish

Put the prepared mussels in a large saucepan. Add 1¼ cups water, bring to a boil, cover and cook quickly for 5 minutes, shaking the pan occasionally during the cooking. Add the cockles and continue cooking for a further 3–5 minutes. When the shells open, the shellfish are cooked. Any unopened shells should be discarded. Remove the cockles and mussels from the shells.

Cut the bacon slices in half across the width. Roll each piece neatly and secure with a wooden toothpick. Put in a pan of boiling water for a few minutes to remove the salt and set the rolls. Drain and dry the bacon and discard the toothpicks.

Melt the butter in a large skillet and fry the bacon rolls until brown. Remove from the pan and keep warm. Fry the onion until soft, add the mussels, cockles, and herbs, and season with salt and pepper. Toss in the butter to heat thoroughly. Divide evenly among 4 warm serving plates, scatter the bacon rolls over, and garnish with a sprig of watercress. Serve with Irish Oatcakes (see page 126) and a glass of stout.

COOK'S NOTES
This can be made entirely with either mussels or cockles and served as a main course with boiled potatoes. For a main course serving, double the quantities.

Serves 4
Preparation time: 30 minutes
Cooking time: 8–10 minutes

Fresh Broiled Shrimps with Garlic & Herb Butter

8 whole fresh shrimps in the shell, each weighing no less than 4 oz.

½ cup butter

1 clove garlic, crushed

4 tablespoons mixed herbs, such as parsley, tarragon, and chervil, very finely chopped

salt and pepper

For the garnish:

½ lemon cut into 2 wedges

sprigs of watercress and herbs

Cut the shrimps in half lengthwise, remove the gut and wash under cold running water. Dry with paper towels. Lay the shrimps shell side down on a baking sheet. Blend the butter, garlic, and herbs together and season with pepper and a little salt. Spread the mixture over the shrimps and cook under a preheated, very hot broiler for 3–4 minutes.

Arrange simply on warm plates and garnish with the lemon, sprigs of watercress, and herbs. Serve immediately with Irish Wheaten Bread (see page 128).

Serves 2
Preparation time: 5 minutes
Cooking time: 3–4 minutes

Baked Scallops with Garlic & Herbs

Butter 4 scallop shells or similar size ovenproof dishes with half the butter. Combine the bread crumbs, garlic, and herbs and season with pepper. Divide half this mixture evenly among the containers. Arrange the scallops on top and cover with the remaining crumb mixture and the remaining butter cut into small pieces. Set the shells or dishes on a baking sheet and bake in a preheated oven for approximately 10–12 minutes. Be careful not to overcook the scallops or they will become tough. The wobbly flesh, when cooked, should be only just set. If, when the scallops are cooked, the crumbs aren't golden in color, quickly put the dishes under a hot broiler to finish.

Serve very hot, garnished with lemon wedges and watercress sprigs and accompanied by Irish Wheaten Bread (see page 128).

COOK'S NOTES
Scallops can be bought either fresh or frozen. If bought fresh, ask that they be cleaned for you, reserving the shells. These make wonderful containers for many seafood dishes. You will be left with the nut of white meat and the crescent-shaped orange/pink roe or coral.

Serves 4
Preparation time: 10 minutes
Cooking time: 10–12 minutes
Oven temperature: 425°F

½ cup butter

2 oz. fresh white bread crumbs

1 clove garlic, finely chopped

1 tablespoon finely chopped parsley

1 tablespoon finely chopped cilantro

8 large scallops, shelled, cleaned, and both the white and coral sliced in rings

pepper

For the garnish:

1 lemon, cut into 4 wedges

4 sprigs of watercress

Oysters & Stout

The most popular way of eating oysters has always been in their raw state, fresh from the shell, sometimes with a squeeze of lemon, sometimes with a little cayenne pepper, but always washed down with a glass of creamy stout.

6–12 fresh, tightly closed oysters, washed and scrubbed

crushed ice

For serving:

1–2 thick lemon wedges

cayenne pepper (optional)

Irish Wheaten Bread (see page 128)

butter, for the bread

glass of stout

Open the oysters just before serving by holding each one firmly in a thick cloth. Insert a strong sharp knife, an old-fashioned pointed can opener, or a screwdriver into the hinge of the shell. Give a sharp twist upward and pry off the shell. If you have difficulty opening the oysters from the hinge, try to pry the shells open by inserting the knife at the side of the shell. Take care not to lose the oyster juices.

Loosen the oyster, leaving it in the deep half of the shell which has retained the juices. Arrange the oysters on a bed of crushed ice on a large serving plate. Serve with lemon wedges, a dusting of cayenne pepper, if desired, buttered wheaten bread, and a glass of creamy stout.

Cook's Notes
Oysters should be eaten like this only when bought fresh and alive. The shells should be tightly closed and can be stored for several days if carefully packed in ice and well refrigerated.

Serves 1–2
Preparation time: 5 minutes

The secret will never be known,

She cannot discover,

The breath of her lover,

But thinks it as sweet as her own.

(JONATHAN SWIFT)

Irish Smoked Salmon with Potato Cakes, Sour Cream & Chives

8 oz. potatoes, boiled and mashed

pinch salt

2 tablespoons butter, melted

½ cup all-purpose flour, plus extra for shaping and cooking

snipped chives, to garnish

For serving:

8–10 oz. smoked salmon, thinly sliced

2 tomatoes (seeds removed), diced

4 tablespoons thick sour cream

First prepare the potato cakes. Put all the ingredients into a bowl and mix gently with a wooden spoon to form a light dough. Place on a lightly floured surface and roll into a circle about ½-inch thick. Cut into 4 circles using a 2½-inch cookie cutter.

Warm a heavy skillet over a gentle heat until a light dusting of flour just begins to turn a very pale fawn color. Keep the pan at this temperature and add the potato cakes. Cook for a few minutes until lightly browned on each side.

While the potato cakes are cooking, divide the salmon among 4 serving plates, arranging it on one side. Allow the potato cakes to cool slightly. Place one on each plate beside the salmon. Arrange the tomato on top of each potato cake, top with sour cream, and garnish with chives. Serve immediately.

COOK'S NOTES
You can double quantities of the ingredients given for the potato cakes and use the extra potato cakes for serving with bacon and eggs as part of an Ulster Fry (see page 58). They are also good eaten hot with butter and homemade jam.

Serves 4
Preparation time: 10 minutes
Cooking time: 8 minutes

Irish Smoked Salmon with Wheaten Bread

I believe that there is only one way to eat the best smoked salmon, and that is cut in generous slices with the finest wheaten bread—naturally, both from Ireland.

Arrange the smoked salmon slices on 4 serving plates. Serve with buttered wheaten bread and garnish with a lemon wedge.

Freshly ground black pepper, finely chopped onion, and capers are the traditional garnish, but I think, with such a fine product, the delicate taste of the fish should not be overpowered by additions.

COOK'S NOTES

Smoked salmon can be bought already sliced in prepared packs; in whole sides, sliced or unsliced; or cut to order from delicatessens and fish markets. When presliced it is generally cut thinly; when cutting it yourself, more generous slices can be allowed. Good quality smoked salmon should be moist and delicate in color.

You can make a quick smoked salmon pâté by mixing equal quantities of smoked salmon pieces or trimmings with curd or soft cheese in a food processor with lemon juice and black pepper. Allow 2 oz. salmon and 2 oz. cheese per portion.

Serves 4
Preparation time: 5 minutes

8–10 oz. Irish smoked salmon, sliced

Irish Wheaten Bread (see page 128)

butter, for the bread

1 lemon, quartered into wedges

Irish Smoked Salmon with Scrambled Eggs

1 tablespoon butter

3 large eggs

1 tablespoon milk

1 tablespoon cream (optional)

1–1½ oz. smoked salmon, cut into narrow strips

1 teaspoon finely snipped chives

1–2 slices warm wheaten bread, toasted and buttered

salt and pepper

Place the eggs in a bowl and mix well with a fork. Add the milk and season with salt and pepper. Melt the butter in a saucepan until foaming. Pour the eggs into the foaming butter. Stir with a wooden spoon over gentle heat, scraping the bottom of the pan and bringing the outside edges to the middle. The scrambled eggs are cooked when they form soft, creamy curds and are barely set. Remove from the heat, stir in the cream, salmon, and chives and pile onto the hot, brown toast on a warm serving plate. Serve immediately.

COOK'S NOTES

Salmon slices, trimmings, or off-cuts are excellent for this dish and dill makes an interesting alternative to the chives.

Serves 1
Preparation time: 5 minutes
Cooking time: 3–4 minutes

fish & seafood

Ireland's crystal clear rivers and streams, and the seas which surround the island, have always been a rich source of food for the people. Whether it be salmon, the king of fish, the humble herring, the noble oyster, or the simple cockle, there has always been an abundant supply to be had for the fishing or the taking. The fish were simply poached to retain the best of their character, flavor, and appearance, or added to a meat pie or tart to feed a large family.

Cod & Shrimp Bake in Cheese Sauce

1½ cups milk

¼ of an onion

6 peppercorns

blade of mace

bay leaf

a few parsley sprigs

¼ cup butter

1 lb. cod fillets, skin and bones removed

2 oz. button mushrooms, sliced

4 oz. cooked, peeled shrimps

¼ cup plus 2 tablespoons flour

1 tablespoon lemon juice

4 oz. grated cheddar cheese

salt and pepper

Put the milk into a saucepan with the onion, peppercorns, blade of mace, bay leaf, and parsley sprigs. Bring to a boil, then remove from the heat and leave to steep while preparing the remaining ingredients.

Melt the butter in another saucepan and use a little to brush the inside of a 2 quart ovenproof pie dish. Cut the cod into finger-size strips, place in the pie dish, and scatter the mushrooms and shrimps on top. Strain the milk, then discard the contents of the strainer. Add the flour to the remaining butter in the saucepan, stirring to blend. Gradually stir in the strained milk to make a smooth sauce. Bring to a boil, stirring constantly until the sauce thickens. Season with salt, pepper, and lemon juice and add two thirds of the grated cheese. Stir until melted. Pour the sauce over the fish, sprinkle with the remaining cheese, place on a baking sheet and cook in a preheated oven for 20–25 minutes until golden-brown. Serve with Irish Wheaten Bread (see page 128) and salad.

COOK'S NOTES
Any firm fleshed fish or shellfish can be used for this dish along with cultivated or wild mushrooms. The bake can also be made in 4 individual pie dishes, each holding approximately 1 cup, or in 8 scallop shells. This makes an excellent appetizer.

Serves 4
Preparation time: 15 minutes
Cooking time: 20–25 minutes
Cooking temperature: 350°F

Creamy Salmon Kedgeree

¼ cup butter

1 large onion, finely chopped

6 oz. long grain rice, cooked until just tender

1 lb. cooked salmon (bones removed), broken into large flakes

3 hard-boiled eggs, roughly chopped

2 tablespoons finely chopped parsley

⅔ cup light cream

salt and pepper

1 teaspoon finely chopped chives, to garnish

Melt half the butter in a large pan and fry the onion until soft. Stir in the rice and season well with salt and pepper. Add the salmon, eggs, parsley, and cream, folding them carefully into the rice to prevent the fish and eggs from breaking up too much. Pile into an ovenproof dish, cover with buttered foil, and heat thoroughly in a preheated oven for 15 minutes. When hot, serve sprinkled with the chives.

COOK'S NOTES

Any white fish such as haddock or smoked fish can also be used to make the kedgeree. A combination of fresh and smoked salmon is particularly good.

The light cream can be omitted, but it helps to keep the dish moist.

A curry sauce is sometimes added for moisture and additional flavor.

Serves 4
Preparation time: 15 minutes
Cooking time: 15 minutes
Oven temperature: 350°F

Baked Trout with Herb Stuffing & Cream Sauce

Melt 4 tablespoons of the butter in a large skillet and fry the onion until soft but not brown. Remove from the heat. Mix the herbs together and add half to the pan along with the bread crumbs, lemon rind, juice, and nutmeg. Season with salt and pepper. Mix well and moisten with 1–2 tablespoons of the cream. Divide this mixture equally among the 4 fish, using it to stuff the belly of each.

Butter a large ovenproof baking dish with half the remaining butter. Lay the stuffed trout head to tail in the baking dish, dot with the remaining butter, and pour the wine over, if using. Bake in a preheated oven for 20 minutes until slightly firm to the touch. Pour the cooking liquor into a saucepan and boil rapidly, reducing by half. Add the remaining cream and herbs and return to a boil, adjusting the seasoning if necessary.

Arrange the fish on individual warm serving plates and pour a little sauce over each fish. Serve with boiled potatoes and crisp green vegetables or salad.

COOK'S NOTES
Brown trout are a wild freshwater fish, native to Ireland and found in the rivers, lakes, and streams throughout the country. They are a fine delicate fish with a slightly nutty flavor.

Serves 4
Preparation time: 20 minutes
Cooking time: 20 minutes
Cooking temperature: 475°F

6 tablespoons butter

1 small onion, finely chopped

2 tablespoons finely chopped parsley

1 tablespoon finely chopped chives

3 teaspoons finely chopped dill

2 oz. fine white bread crumbs

finely grated rind of ½ lemon

2 teaspoons lemon juice

pinch nutmeg

1 cup light cream

4 rainbow or brown trout, approximately 10–11 oz. each, cleaned

⅔ cup dry white wine (optional)

salt and pepper

Fried Trout with Toasted Hazelnuts & Herbs

4 trout, approximately 10–11 oz. each, gutted, washed, and dried, heads and tails left on

1 cup all-purpose flour

1 stick butter, clarified (see Cook's Notes)

1 stick butter, melted

4 oz. hazelnuts, shelled

2 tablespoons lemon juice

2 tablespoons finely chopped parsley

1 tablespoon finely chopped chives

salt and pepper

For the garnish:

1 lemon, cut into 4 wedges

watercress sprigs

Season the fish well, inside and out, and toss in the flour, shaking off the excess. Fry in the clarified butter (see Cook's Notes) until golden brown, about 5 minutes on each side, turning once very carefully to prevent the skin from breaking.

While the trout are cooking, toast the hazelnuts under the broiler until the skins can be rubbed off easily, then chop roughly. Quickly melt the remaining butter in a small pan, allow it to foam and turn brown, then add the lemon juice. Transfer the cooked trout to 4 warm serving plates. Scatter the nuts on top of each trout and keep warm. Pour the browned butter on top of the fish. Scatter the herbs on top and garnish with lemon wedges and watercress. Serve with boiled new potatoes and a green vegetable or a salad.

COOK'S NOTES
To clarify butter: put the butter in a small saucepan, bring to a boil, and let it bubble several times without browning. Remove from the heat and allow to settle. Carefully pour through a strainer lined with damp cheesecloth. This will catch all the salty sediment which causes butter to burn.

Serves 4
Preparation time: 10–15 minutes
Cooking time: 6–8 minutes

Grilled Salmon Steaks with Herb Butter

Mix the butter, herbs, and lemon juice in a bowl. Lay the butter on a piece of waxed paper and roll into a log shape about 1 inch in diameter. Refrigerate until solid.

Wash and dry the salmon steaks. Brush a baking sheet with melted butter and lay the steaks on top. Brush with half of the remaining butter and season well with salt and pepper. Cook under a preheated medium broiler for about 4–5 minutes on each side. On turning each steak, brush with more melted butter and season again. Alternatively, the steaks can be cooked on a cast-iron skillet.

Cut the log of herb butter into four circles. Transfer the cooked steaks carefully onto warm plates and top each with a circle of butter. Garnish with lemon wedges and sprigs of watercress and serve with boiled new potatoes, steamed vegetables, or a green salad.

COOK'S NOTES

For ease of eating, the skin and central bones of the steaks can be removed before serving, but this needs to be done with care; otherwise the fish can lose its shape. It is best done on the serving plate, removing the skin and bones before the fish is garnished and served.

Serves 4
Preparation time: 15 minutes
Cooking time: 8–10 minutes

1 stick butter

2 tablespoons mixed herbs such as parsley, dill, chervil, chives, or fennel, very finely chopped

squeeze of lemon juice

4 salmon steaks about 6–8 oz. each (¾–1 inch thick)

¼ cup butter, melted

salt and pepper

For the garnish:

4 lemon wedges

sprigs of watercress

Roast Fillet of Salmon with Saffron Cream Sauce

4 salmon fillets, about
5–6 oz. each

oil, for frying and roasting

salt and pepper

1–2 tablespoons finely
snipped chives, to garnish

For the sauce:

⅔ cup fish stock (see
Cook's Notes)

⅔ cup dry white wine

4 strands saffron

⅔ cup light cream

Season the salmon with salt and pepper. Heat a little oil in a large skillet until hot, and place the salmon in the pan flesh side down. Cook for about 2 minutes over high heat to brown. Transfer the salmon to a lightly greased baking sheet, skin side down. Season and finish cooking in a preheated oven for about 7–9 minutes, depending on the thickness of the fillet. The flesh should be pink and opaque when cooked.

While the fish is roasting, make the sauce by combining the stock, wine, and saffron in a saucepan. Bring to a boil, reduce the heat, and simmer until reduced by half. Add the cream, bring to a boil, and boil continuously until the sauce thickens and coats the back of a spoon.

Serve the fish in the center of a large plate with the sauce poured around and garnished with chives. Accompany with steamed seasonal vegetables and boiled new potatoes.

COOK'S NOTES
Fish Stock: for 5 cups stock, sauté 8 oz. chopped white vegetables in butter until soft, add 1 lb. washed white fish bones and trimmings. Pour in ⅔ cup dry white wine, 4½ cups water, and the juice of 1 lemon. Simmer for 20 minutes and strain before use.

Serves 2
Preparation time: 2–5 minutes
Cooking time: 9–11 minutes
Oven temperature: 475°F

Salmon Fish Cakes

Combine the potatoes, flaked fish, Tabasco sauce or cayenne pepper, lemon juice, and parsley in a large bowl and season well with salt and pepper; mix well to combine. Bind with the egg yolk. Turn the mixture onto a lightly floured surface and form into a thick roll about 11 inches long and 2 inches thick. Cut into 8 equal size pieces and shape each into neat cakes approximately 3 oz. in weight, 2½ inches in diameter, and ¾ inch thick.

Dip the cakes in the beaten egg and coat evenly with bread crumbs. Place the oil and butter in a skillet and fry the fish cakes for approximately 5 minutes on each side until they are crisp, golden and very hot. Drain well on paper towels and serve with fresh tomato sauce and lemon wedges.

COOK'S NOTES

Fish cakes in Ireland were traditionally made with salmon because it was free for the catching. Today, however, since salmon is more expensive, any white fish such as cod, haddock, or whiting may be substituted. A combination of smoked and fresh fish is also good.

Serves 4
Preparation time: 20 minutes
Cooking time: 10 minutes

8 oz. cooked, mashed potatoes

1 lb. salmon, cooked, skinned, and flaked

few drops Tabasco sauce or ½ teaspoon cayenne pepper (optional)

1–2 tablespoons lemon juice

2 tablespoons finely chopped parsley

1 large egg yolk, beaten

flour, for dusting

1 large egg, beaten

4–6 oz. fresh white bread crumbs

1 tablespoon oil

¼ cup butter

salt and pepper

For serving:

fresh tomato sauce

4 lemon wedges

Steamed Mussels in White Wine Sauce

¼ cup butter

1 large onion, finely chopped

1–2 cloves garlic, finely chopped

1 small leek, white and green parts, finely sliced

4 lbs. live mussels, prepared (see Cook's Notes, page 19)

1¼ cup dry white wine

¼ cup flour

2 tablespoons finely chopped parsley

1-2 tablespoons heavy cream (optional)

salt and pepper

Melt half the butter in a very large saucepan and gently fry the onion, garlic, and leek until soft but not brown. Add the mussels, white wine, and ⅔ cup water, cover and bring to a boil. Cook for 2–5 minutes until the mussels open, shaking the pan several times during the cooking. Using a slotted spoon, divide the mussels among 4 large soup plates, discarding any that haven't opened during cooking. Keep warm.

Mix the remaining butter with the flour to form a paste and gradually add to the juices in the pan, stirring to thicken. Bring to a boil, season to taste, stir in the parsley, and pour over the mussels. Serve immediately with wheaten or soda bread. Just before serving, 1–2 tablespoons heavy cream can be added to the sauce for extra richness, if you like.

COOK'S NOTES
Allow about 1 lb. mussels per person, about 15–20 mussels if you are fortunate enough to be able to gather them yourself. For cooking I use a large saucepan, shaking and turning the mussels continually, bringing those nearest the heat to the top of the pile to ensure that they all cook quickly and evenly.

Serves 4
Preparation time: 15 minutes
Cooking time: 8 minutes

God be with the happy times,

When the troubles we had not,

And our mothers made colcannon,

In the three-legged pot. (Traditional Rhyme)

Dressed Crab

Traditionally, crabs and other shellfish were gathered by the locals from the many bays along the coast. Eaten in greater quantity, they were once the main source of protein for coastal dwellers. Today they are enjoyed as an affordable luxury, most often eaten as Dressed Crab and served with salad.

1 live crab, approximately 1¾ lbs.

2–3 tablespoons fine white bread crumbs

¼–½ teaspoon dry mustard

salt and pepper

squeeze of lemon juice

For the garnish:

1 hard-boiled egg, white chopped, yolk finely chopped

1–2 tablespoons finely chopped parsley

sprigs of watercress

lemon wedges

Plunge the crab into a large pan of boiling salted water. Cover and simmer for 25 minutes. Remove from the water and leave to cool.

Lay the crab on its back and twist off the legs and claws. Remove the bony tail flap and discard. Pry off the central body, pulling it free from the shell. This consists of bone with some white crab meat and the "dead men's fingers." Discard the "fingers," the stomach sac from behind the mouth, and the mouth itself. Cut the body in half and using a skewer, pick out the white meat from the crevices. Put into a bowl. Scoop out the soft, yellowish-brown meat from inside the shell and place in a second bowl. Crack the claws and legs, extract the meat, and combine with the reserved white meat. Cream the brown meat, add the bread crumbs and mustard. Season with salt and pepper. Arrange down the center of the washed and dried shell. Season the white meat with salt, pepper, and lemon juice, and pile on either side of the brown meat. Garnish with the egg, parsley, watercress, and lemon and serve with mayonnaise, wheaten bread, and salad.

COOK'S NOTES

It is always best to cook your own crab. They not only have a better flavor, but you know they are fresh. If only cooked crabs are available, buy them from a reputable fish market.

Small heavy crabs will have plenty of meat. To use the shell as a container, enlarge the opening by breaking away the shell along the line of weakness that runs around the shell's rim.

Serves 1
Preparation time: 30 minutes
Cooking time: 25 minutes

Cold Boiled Lobster with Herb Mayonnaise

Remove the claws from the lobster, crack, and reserve. Extend the lobster's tail, shell side down and cut in half through its length. Discard the stomach sac in the head, the feathery gills, and the dark intestinal vein running down the center of the tail. Rub the grayish-green liver and the pink roe through a strainer into a mixing bowl, add the remaining ingredients, and stir to combine.

Remove the flesh from the tail shells and cut into diagonal slices. Put into a bowl and add enough of the mayonnaise mixture to moisten. Return the lobster meat to the shell halves. Add a little extra mayonnaise for appearance.

Arrange a half lobster on each plate, garnish with a cracked claw, lemon wedge, and watercress. Serve with a mixed green salad, the remaining herb mayonnaise, and buttered wheaten bread.

COOK'S NOTES

When buying any cooked shellfish it is important that they are very fresh. If possible, buy them live and cook them yourself. To cook a lobster, plunge it head first into rapidly boiling, salted water. Hold down with tongs and boil for 1½ minutes. Reduce the heat and simmer for 8–10 minutes per pound to cook the flesh.

Serves 2
Preparation time: 15–20 minutes

1 cooked lobster, approximately 2 lbs. (see Cook's Notes)

1 hard-boiled egg, grated

2 tablespoons finely chopped parsley

2 tablespoons finely chopped chervil

1 teaspoon finely chopped chives

1 tablespoon finely chopped capers

⅔ cup thick mayonnaise

lemon juice, to taste

For the garnish:

2 lemon wedges

sprigs of watercress

Dublin Lawyer

At one time, lobster, along with other forms of shellfish, were a popular food with those who could catch them. Today they are much less readily available, and this, coupled with increasing demand from restaurants, has made them a luxury item commanding premium prices.

1 live lobster, approximately 2 lbs.

¼ cup butter

1 small onion, finely chopped

4 tablespoons Irish whiskey

⅔ cup heavy cream

1 teaspoon dry mustard

1 teaspoon lemon juice

salt and pepper

For the garnish:

sprigs of watercress

lemon wedges

Plunge the lobster, head first, into rapidly boiling salted water for 2 minutes. Remove and hold under cold running water to stop the cooking. Set the lobster on a chopping board shell side down, extend the lobster's tail and cut lengthwise through the center, dividing it in two. Discard the stomach sac in the head, the feathery gills, and the dark intestinal vein running down the center of the tail. Remove the meat from the shells and cut into chunks. Crack the claws and remove the meat.

Heat the butter in a large skillet and fry the onion until soft. Add the lobster meat and fry until just cooked, then add the coral and liver. Warm the whiskey, pour over, and carefully ignite. When the flames have died down, add the rest of the ingredients and mix well. Put the lobster meat in the warm shells. Boil the liquid to reduce and thicken, pour it over the lobster, and serve immediately garnished with watercress and lemon wedges.

Serves 2
Preparation time: 20–30 minutes
Cooking time: 20 minutes

Grilled Mackerel with Gooseberry & Fennel Sauce

Season the mackerel inside and out and stuff with the fennel sprigs and stalks. Cut 2–3 diagonal slits on each side of the backbone so that the heat can penetrate more quickly. Brush both the fish and a baking sheet lightly with oil and set the prepared fish on top.

Prepare the sauce by combining the gooseberries with ½ cup water in a large saucepan. Bring to a boil and add the sugar, butter, and fennel. Cook gently for 6–7 minutes until the berries burst but still have texture.

While the sauce is cooking, place the mackerel under a preheated broiler and cook for 4–7 minutes on each side, depending on the size, turning very carefully. Remove the herb stuffing and serve immediately, garnished with lemon wedges and sprigs of fennel. Accompany with the hot gooseberry sauce and boiled new potatoes.

COOK'S NOTES

Mackerel, being a very oily fish, needs a sharp sauce to offset the richness of the flesh. Gooseberries or other sharp fruit such as rhubarb are traditional, but sorrel and mustard are also popular.

Herrings can also be cooked in this way.

Serves 4
Preparation time: 5–10 minutes
Cooking time: 8–15 minutes

4 small mackerel, approximately 9 oz. each, gutted, washed, and dried

fresh fennel sprigs, fronds and stalks (optional)

oil, for brushing

For the sauce:

12 oz. gooseberries, stems and bottoms removed

2 tablespoons sugar

2 tablespoons butter

1 tablespoon finely chopped fennel

salt and pepper

For the garnish:

4 lemon wedges

4 sprigs of fennel

Herb Stuffed Herring with Mustard Sauce

4 herring, approximately 4 oz. each, prepared (see Cook's Notes)

For the stuffing:

6 tablespoons butter

1 small onion, finely chopped

2 tablespoons parsley, finely chopped

1 teaspoon dill, finely chopped

2 hard-boiled eggs, finely chopped

grated rind of ½ lemon

2 oz. bread crumbs

salt and pepper

For the sauce:

2 tablespoons butter

¼ cup flour

1¼ cups milk

1 tablespoon lemon juice

1 tablespoon prepared dry mustard

1 tablespoon finely chopped parsley

For the garnish:

4 lemon wedges

4 sprigs of flat leaf parsley

To make the stuffing, melt half the butter in a saucepan and fry the onion until soft. Use the rest of the butter to grease an ovenproof dish and a sheet of foil. Add the remaining stuffing ingredients to the onion and season well to taste. Divide the stuffing among the 4 fish, reshaping them carefully, to make sure the stuffing doesn't fall out. Lay each herring carefully in the dish, cover with the buttered foil, and bake in a preheated oven for 40–45 minutes.

While the fish is baking, prepare the sauce by melting the butter, stirring in the flour and gradually adding the milk to form a smooth paste. Cook gently for about 5 minutes, stirring constantly, until the sauce is thick and the flour cooked. Stir in the lemon juice, mustard, and parsley. Season to taste.

Serve the herring with lemon wedges, flat leaf parsley, the hot mustard sauce, and boiled new potatoes.

COOK'S NOTES

To prepare a herring, scrape off the scales from tail to head. Cut off the fins and gut, slitting the belly from behind the head to the vent. Pull out the viscera. Run the point of a knife down the backbone to release any blood and wash under cold running water. Dry well.

Serves 4–8

Preparation time: 15–20 minutes
Cooking time: 40–45 minutes
Oven temperature: 325°F

Fried Herring in Mustard & Oatmeal

Spread a little mustard inside each herring. Dip in the beaten egg and roll each herring in the seasoned oatmeal, pressing it evenly over the fish.

Heat the fat or oil in a large skillet and cook the herring gently for about 4 minutes on each side until an even golden-brown. Drain on paper towels, garnish with lemon wedges and watercress, and serve with boiled new potatoes.

COOK'S NOTES

If the herring are small, allow 2 per person. Although it is traditional to serve the herring with the heads on, they can be removed before cooking. The backbone can also be removed and the herring flattened before being coated and fried. Fry the flesh side first if using this method.

Herring can be bought already prepared from the supermarket, delicatessen, or fish market. When scraping the scales from the fish, work from the tail end to the head. Cut off the fins with a pair of kitchen scissors. The herring can be prepared more simply by omitting the egg, mustard, and oatmeal and dipping in flour before frying.

Serves 4

Preparation time: 15 minutes
Cooking time: 8–10 minutes

4 herring, approximately 4 oz. each, gutted, scaled, fins removed, washed, and dried

1–2 tablespoons prepared dry mustard

1 egg, beaten

3 oz. oatmeal, seasoned with salt and pepper

bacon fat or oil, for frying

salt and pepper

For the garnish:

1 lemon, cut in wedges

sprigs of watercress

Smoked Fish Pie

A favorite in many Irish homes on a Friday, where the tradition of not eating meat on this day is still practiced. Fish pie can be made with plain white fish or a combination of smoked and white fish.

1 lb. smoked haddock

1½ cups milk

¼ cup butter

1 onion, finely chopped

6 oz. mushrooms, sliced

¼ cup flour

1 teaspoon prepared dry mustard

2 tablespoons finely chopped parsley

1 tablespoon lemon juice

2–3 eggs, hard-boiled and roughly chopped

salt and pepper

For the topping:

1¾ lb. potatoes, cooked and mashed

2 tablespoons butter, melted

3–4 tablespoons milk

2 oz. cheddar cheese, grated

Put the haddock in a shallow saucepan, pour on the milk, heat slowly until simmering and cook for 5–10 minutes.

Meanwhile, melt the butter in a pan and fry the onion until soft but not brown. Add the mushrooms and continue to fry until coloring. Stir in the flour and cook gently for about 1 minute. Remove from the heat.

When the fish is cooked, strain the liquor into a pitcher and gradually add it to the onion and mushroom mixture, stirring well. Bring to a boil and simmer for 10 minutes until thick, stirring constantly. Add the mustard, parsley, lemon juice, and eggs. Season with salt and pepper. Flake the fish, remove the bones, and add to the sauce. Pour into a deep ovenproof pie dish.

Mix the potatoes with the melted butter and milk, season well and pile roughly on top of the fish mixture, covering it evenly. Scatter the cheese on top and bake in a preheated oven for about 30 minutes until piping hot and crisp.

COOK'S NOTES
When using smoked fish in this or any other recipe, buy naturally smoked, undyed fish. The best quality smoked haddock is finnan haddie. For extra flavor, add 6 peppercorns, a blade of mace, 1 bay leaf, 1 wedge of onion, and 2 cloves to the milk, while cooking the fish.

Serves 4–6
Preparation time: 20–30 minutes
Cooking time: 35–40 minutes
Oven temperature: 375°F

meat

Although cattle were originally bred mainly for their milk, and sheep for their wool, their meat was highly prized by the country's kings and noblemen and was served at formal banquets and feasts. Its importance was such that the rank and status of the guests was determined by the cuts of roast meat that they were offered. Today, beef and lamb are still important elements of the meal in most households. Pork and bacon have always been less expensive and therefore more accessible.

An Ulster Fry

This is one of Ireland's most famous dishes. It differs from a Scottish or English "fry" in that it is served with a selection of fried Irish breads: potato bread, soda bread, and dropped scones. It also commonly includes fried black and white puddings.

oil, for frying

1–2 sausages

2 bacon slices

2 slices black or white pudding

½ Soda Farl (see page 124)

1 Potato Bread, halved (see page 129)

1 Drop Scone (see page 137)

1 tomato, halved

1–2 eggs

sprigs of watercress, to garnish

Heat a little oil and fry the sausages until almost cooked, then add the bacon slices and black or white pudding and continue to fry. Remove from the pan and drain on a plate lined with paper towels. Keep warm. Fry the soda bread and potato bread until lightly toasted. Drain and keep warm. Fry the tomato halves, skin side down until softened but still holding their shape. Remove and keep warm. Add a little extra oil to the pan, heat and fry the egg or eggs, spooning the hot fat over the yolk and the white until cooked to your liking. Arrange all the fried ingredients on a hot plate, garnish with the sprigs of watercress and serve immediately.

COOK'S NOTES
An Ulster Fry can be served at any time of the day: for breakfast, lunch, supper, or as a snack. Mushrooms, onions, liver, chops, and fried potatoes can also be added if a more substantial meal is required!

Serves 1
Preparation time: 5 minutes
Cooking time: 15 minutes

Pork Ribs & Onions

2 lbs. pork spare ribs

2½ cups water or stock

2 large onions, sliced

1 bay leaf, parsley sprigs, 1 stalk of celery, and 1 blade of mace tied together

1 tablespoon corn flour (available in health food stores)

2 tablespoons finely chopped parsley

salt and pepper

Wash the ribs and cut into manageable sized portions. Put into a large saucepan and add the water or stock. Bring to a boil and skim. Add the onions, herbs, and season with salt and pepper. Cover, reduce the heat and simmer for 2–2½ hours until the pork is tender and beginning to fall from the bone. Blend the corn flour with a little of the cooking liquid, then return to the pan to thicken. Add the parsley, taste and adjust the seasoning if necessary, and serve with boiled potatoes and a glass of stout.

Serves 4
Preparation time: 5 minutes
Cooking time: 2–2½ hours

Roast Stuffed Pork Chops

¼ cup butter

1 large onion, finely chopped

6 oz. fresh white bread crumbs

grated rind of ½ lemon

pinch dried thyme

1½ tablespoons finely chopped parsley

a little beaten egg to bind

2 boneless pork chops of even size, approximately 12 oz. each

salt and pepper

For the gravy:

1 tablespoon arrowroot

1¼ cups stock

Melt half the butter in a pan and fry the onion until soft but not brown. Stir in the bread crumbs, lemon rind, herbs, and season to taste. Use a little beaten egg to bind. Allow to cool.

Slit the pork chops lengthwise without cutting through them and flatten the meat until the chops lie flat. Arrange the stuffing on top of one of the chops, turning in the tails at both ends. Lay the second chop on top, also tucking in the ends and wrapping the long sides around to encase the stuffing. Tie at intervals with string. Heat the remaining butter in an ovenproof dish and brown the chops. Pour on ⅔ cup water, cover tightly and cook in a preheated oven for 1–1¼ hours. Remove the string and transfer to a warm serving dish. Thicken the cooking juices with the arrowroot blended in the stock, and taste and adjust the seasoning if necessary. Serve the chops carved in slices and accompanied by applesauce.

Serves 4
Preparation time: 30 minutes
Cooking time: 1–1¼ hours
Oven temperature: 350°F

Lamb's Liver with Bacon & Onions

Place a little oil in a pan and fry the bacon until brown and beginning to crisp. Remove from the pan and keep warm. Fry the onion in the remaining fat until soft and just beginning to color. Remove from the pan and keep warm with the bacon. Place the flour in a large plastic bag and season with salt and pepper. Add the slices of liver, one at a time, to the flour, coating evenly and shaking off any excess. Add a little extra oil to the pan and quickly fry the liver until brown on both sides and cooked through. Divide the liver, bacon, and onions between 2 serving plates and serve immediately with Champ (see page 101).

a little oil, for frying

4 slices bacon

1 large onion, sliced

2 tablespoons flour

1 lb. lamb's liver, sliced

salt and pepper

Serves 2
Preparation time: 10 minutes
Cooking time: 10–15 minutes

Pressed Ox Tongue

Put the tongue in a pan, cover with water and bring to a boil. Drain and rinse, return to the pan and cover with water. Add the onion (stuck with cloves), peppercorns, carrot, celery, and herbs. Bring to a boil and simmer for 4 hours. Cool slightly in the liquid, strain and reserve the liquid. Remove the tongue and plunge into cold water. Remove the skin, root, and small bones. Curl the tongue to fit into a tongue press or straight-sided dish.

Mix the gelatin in an ovenproof bowl with a little cold water, then set in a saucepan of hot water. Stir and melt until clear, and add to the reserved liquid. Pour the liquid over the tongue, cover, and weigh down to press. Leave in the refrigerator overnight to set before removing from the dish. Slice thinly to serve.

1 salted ox tongue, 3–6 lbs., soaked in cold water overnight

1 large onion, stuck with 5 cloves

6–8 peppercorns

1 large carrot, halved

2 celery stalks, halved

2 bay leaves

a few parsley sprigs and a sprig of thyme

2 teaspoons powdered gelatin

Serves 6
Preparation time: 10–15 minutes
Cooking time: 4–5 hours, plus soaking overnight and pressing overnight

Baked Irish Ham

Until recent years, pork and bacon were central to the diet of the Irish. As a result, there is a wide variety of traditional recipes for the various cuts of pork. The sides of the pig were known as the "flitch" and cured as bacon, whereas the hind legs were cured as ham.

4 lb. joint of bacon or ham, cooked and rind removed (see Boiled Bacon and Cabbage, right)

4 tablespoons light brown sugar

whole cloves

⅔ cup ham stock

Set the cooked joint in a roasting pan. Mark a diamond pattern over the fat with a knife at 1–1½-inch intervals. Press the light brown sugar into the fat, completely covering the top and sides. Stick a clove in the center of each diamond. Pour the stock into the roasting dish around the joint. Cook in a preheated oven for 20 minutes until the fat is crisp and brown. Serve carved in slices (you will get 10–12) with roast potatoes or Champ (see page 101), boiled cabbage wedges, braised red cabbage, cauliflower, carrots, celery, or leeks.

COOK'S NOTES
If the joint of bacon or ham is cold, use a lower oven temperature, 350°F, and bake for 30–45 minutes.

Serves 6–8
Preparation time: 5–10 minutes
Cooking time: 20 minutes
Oven temperature: 425°F

Boiled Bacon & Cabbage

Drain the bacon, put into a large saucepan, cover with fresh cold water, and bring to a boil. Discard the water, rinse the bacon, wash out the pan and begin again with fresh water, adding all the ingredients except the cabbage. Bring to a boil, cover the pan and simmer for 25 minutes per pound.

Add the cabbage wedges 20–25 minutes before the end of the cooking time and continue to cook until the bacon and cabbage are tender. Remove the bacon and cabbage from the cooking liquid and drain the cabbage well. Peel the rind from the bacon and serve the bacon in slices with the cabbage wedges, boiled potatoes, and parsley sauce.

COOK'S NOTES
A 4 lb. joint of bacon when cooked will yield approximately 10–20 slices, depending on whether the meat is carved hot or cold, plus a 5 oz. tail piece, which makes an ideal meat pie filling.

Serves 6–8
Preparation time: 10–15 minutes, plus soaking overnight
Cooking time: 1 hour 40 minutes

. . and the kale and praties blended

Like the pictures in a dream. (TRADITIONAL RHYME)

4 lb. joint of bacon, smoked or unsmoked, tied in a neat shape and soaked overnight in cold water

1 onion, quartered

2 carrots, quartered

2 celery, stalks, quartered

1 leek, quartered

2 bay leaves, sprig thyme, parsley sprigs, and blade of mace tied together

10 peppercorns

1 tight-headed green cabbage, cut into wedges, core removed, for serving

Irish Spiced Beef

4–6 lbs. beef, top round or flank steak

selection of flavorings, such as onions, parsnips, turnips, carrots, celery, and a bunch of herbs

1¼ cups stout (optional)

For the pickle:

5 teaspoons crushed bay leaves

2 teaspoons ground cloves

3 teaspoons ground ginger

3 teaspoons ground mace

1 teaspoon pepper

½ teaspoon ground allspice

4 cloves garlic, crushed

6 tablespoons brown sugar

8 oz. spiced pickling mixture or 1 oz. saltpeter, and 1 lb. coarse salt
6–7 pints cold water

Tie the meat into a neat shape. Combine all the spicing ingredients in a large glass bowl, mix well, and add the meat. Make sure there is enough liquid to cover. Cover and refrigerate for 1 week, turning daily.

When pickled, put into a large pot with the flavorings. Cover with water, bring to a boil, and simmer for 2–2½ hours. During the last 30 minutes of cooking the stout can be added for extra flavor, if you like.

When cooked, remove the meat from the cooking liquor, wrap tightly in waxed paper and foil to set the shape, and allow to cool. Refrigerate overnight before serving carved in slices with pickles.

COOK'S NOTES

Boned and rolled brisket of beef, also known in Ireland as top breast of beef, can be used. It cuts into very neat circular slices, but takes 4–5 hours to cook.

Traditionally saltpeter was used for spicing beef, but it is not always easy to obtain. Spiced pickling mixture, however, which should have the saltpeter already added, can be obtained from your supermarket.

Serves 6–12
Preparation time: begin preparations 1 week before serving
Cooking time: 2–2½ hours

Beef & Stout Stew

Season the flour with salt and pepper and toss the meat in the flour. Heat the oil in a large saucepan or casserole and fry the beef cubes until browned. Add the onion and cook for a few minutes, then stir in any remaining flour. Add the carrot, stout, and 3½ cups water, stirring well to combine. Bring to a boil, add the bay leaf, cover and simmer gently for 1½–2 hours until the meat is tender. Alternatively, cook in a preheated oven for the same length of time.

Half an hour before the end of the cooking time, add the prunes. Remove the bay leaf, taste, and adjust the seasoning if necessary. Sprinkle with the parsley and serve with baked potatoes in their jackets.

COOK'S NOTES

Brisket and beef shank can also be used for this stew, the meat being removed from the bone before cooking. The bone can be tucked down the side of the stew during the cooking, and then removed before serving. This gives additional flavor. Individual slices of meat can also be cooked in this way and are equally delicious.

Serves 4
Preparation time: 20–30 minutes
Cooking time: 1½–2 hours
Oven temperature: 300–325°F

½ cup flour

2 lbs. beef, top round, cut in 1-inch cubes

oil, for frying

1 large onion, peeled and sliced

1 large carrot, peeled and thickly sliced

1¼ cups stout

1 bay leaf

4 oz. pitted prunes, soaked in water

salt and pepper

2 tablespoons finely chopped parsley

Tenderloin Steak with Cashel Blue Cheese & Croutons

2 oz. Cashel Blue cheese

1 tenderloin, approximately 7–8 oz., cut 1½–1¾ inches thick

2 tablespoons butter

¼ oz. croutons (see page 17)

few sprigs of thyme

sprigs of watercress, to garnish

salt and pepper

Trim the rind from the cheese and slice it until you have enough to cover the top of the tenderloin. Season the tenderloin with salt and pepper, and seal on both sides in a little butter in a very hot pan. Transfer to a buttered baking sheet and set the cheese on top. Put into a very hot oven for 5 minutes for rare; 8 for medium-rare, and 15 minutes for well-done, allowing the cheese to melt and lightly brown. Transfer the steak from the baking sheet to a hot plate, scatter the croutons and a few sprigs of thyme, and pour in the cooking juices. Garnish with sprigs of watercress. Serve immediately.

COOK'S NOTES

Cashel Blue is one of Ireland's most famous cheeses and, in addition to being an important element on the cheese board, has many uses in the kitchen. It is perfect in soup, as a topping for toasted bread, scones, and pies, and it can also be used in stuffings for filet mignon and breast of chicken.

Serves 1
Preparation time: 5 minutes
Cooking time: 5–15 minutes
Oven temperature: 425°F

Beef Steak & Oyster Pudding

1½ lbs. top round

½ cup flour, seasoned with salt and pepper

oil, for frying

1 large onion, finely chopped

4 oz. mushrooms, sliced

⅔ cup beef stock

⅔ cup Irish dry stout

1 bay leaf

1–2 tablespoons chopped parsley

12 fresh oysters and their juice

For the pastry:

2 cups flour

1 tablespoon baking powder

4 oz. shredded suet

2 tablespoons butter

salt

Trim the beef and cut into 1-inch cubes. Toss the meat in the seasoned flour and fry until browned. Transfer to a saucepan. Heat the oil and fry the onion until soft. Then add the mushrooms and continue to fry until lightly browned. Add the meat with the stock, stout, bay leaf, and parsley. Bring to a boil, then simmer for 1–1½ hours. Allow the steak pudding filling to cool, then stir in the oysters and their juice. Chill.

Sift the flour, baking powder, and salt into a bowl, mix in the suet, then stir in ⅔ cup water to make a firm dough. Don't overmix or overwork the pastry. Roll out to a circle about 13 inches in diameter. Mark the circle into 4 sections and cut out one triangular wedge. Roll this out to a circle about 7 inches in diameter, for the lid.

Lightly butter a 1½ quart ovenproof dish and line with the pastry to stand 1 inch above the dish. Fill with the steak and oyster mixture. Set the pastry lid on top, brush the rim with water, and fold over the upstanding pastry, pressing to seal together. Cover with a piece of buttered foil and steam in a steamer or pan half-filled with hot water for 1½–1¾ hours, adding boiling water as required.

COOK'S NOTES

2 oz. fresh suet, chopped, and 2 oz. dried shredded suet can be used as an alternative to 4 oz. dried suet. The pastry will benefit from resting and chilling for 30 minutes before using.

If there is too much sauce with the filling, reserve the excess, heat and serve as extra gravy with the pudding.

Serves 4–6

Preparation time: 30 minutes
Cooking time: 1½–2 hours

Ulster Steak

Toss the meat in the seasoned flour. Heat the oil in a large skillet and brown well on all sides. Transfer to a flameproof casserole. Fry the mushrooms for a few minutes to brown slightly, and add to the meat with the onions, the rest of the flour, and other ingredients. Bring to a boil, cover and simmer for 1½–2 hours until the meat is tender. Add a little extra water if the liquid reduces too much—the sauce should be quite liquid and should be "mopped" up with mashed potatoes, champ, or fresh soda bread.

COOK'S NOTES

Seasoned flour is flour to which salt and pepper to flavor has been added.

Sometimes sliced carrots are added to this recipe and stout is used instead of water or stock—both are delicious and quick to prepare.

Serves 4–5
Preparation time: 15–20 minutes
Cooking time: 1½–2 hours

1½–2 lbs. top round, cut into individual portions ¾-inch thick

½ cup flour, seasoned with salt and pepper

oil, for frying

6 oz. button mushrooms

1 large onion, sliced

2 teaspoons mushroom ketchup

1 tablespoon Chinese Bead or brown gravy sauce

3¾ pints water or beef stock

salt and pepper

Gaelic Steak

Heat the butter and oil in a skillet and fry the onion until soft but not brown. Scrape to the side of the pan, increase the heat, and fry the steak on both sides until cooked as required. Remove the meat from the pan and keep warm. Add the whiskey to the pan and ignite. When the flames have subsided, pour in the cream and mix with the onion and meat juices. Bring to a boil, adjust the seasoning, add the parsley, and pour over the meat. Serve immediately garnished with sprigs of watercress.

COOK'S NOTES

A thin slice of sirloin steak can also be used instead of the tenderloin or porterhouse steak. This takes a much shorter time to cook. It is necessary to flame the whiskey to burn off the alcohol and concentrate the flavor. A more pleasant-tasting sauce will result.

Serves 1
Preparation time: 10 minutes
Cooking time: 5–20 minutes

1 tablespoon butter

1 tablespoon oil

3 tablespoons onion, finely chopped

8–10 oz. tenderloin or porterhouse steak, trimmed of excess fat

1 measure (about 2 tablespoons) Irish whiskey

6–8 tablespoons heavy cream

1 tablespoon finely chopped parsley

sprigs of watercress, to garnish

salt and pepper

Ground Beef in Pastry

Beef dishes combined with pastry, such as Steak and Kidney Pie, Ground Beef Tart, and Beef Wellington have been popular in Ireland for many years, as has the versatile Meat Loaf. This family recipe combines elements from them all and is quick and easy to prepare.

1 lb. ground beef

1 small onion, grated

1 clove garlic, crushed

1 small carrot, grated

2 oz. white bread crumbs

1 tablespoon tomato purée

1 tablespoon Worcestershire sauce

1 tablespoon finely chopped parsley

pinch mixed herbs

salt and pepper

For the pastry:

1 lb. frozen puff pastry

flour, for rolling

1 egg, beaten

Combine all the ingredients for the filling, then press into a log shape approximately 3 x 10 inches. Leave to chill in the refrigerator. Roll the pastry thinly to a 12-inch square and cut off a 2-inch strip for decoration. Set the log of meat along the long end of the pastry, brush the edges with a little beaten egg, and fold over the remaining pastry to form a neat package. Press the edges to seal well and finish with a shell pattern or the prongs of a fork. Cut decorations for the top from the pastry strip. Stick these on with beaten egg. Set the pastry log on a baking sheet, brush with beaten egg, and bake in a preheated oven for 45 minutes until golden-brown. Serve hot or cold, cut in slices, with a rich tomato sauce (see Cook's Notes, page 72).

COOK'S NOTES
Four individual portions can be made in the same way, but on a smaller scale. In each case, the onion and carrot needs to be finely grated, as they are uncooked before baking.

Serves 4
Preparation time: 30 minutes
Cooking time: 45 minutes
Oven temperature: 425°F

Boiled Flank Steak with Dumplings

Heat a little oil in a large saucepan, and brown the meat. Add the cloved onion, bunch of herbs, 2½ cups water, and the stout. Bring to a boil, then simmer for 2 hours until the meat is tender. Three quarters of the way through the cooking time, remove the cloved onion and herbs and add the whole vegetables.

Meanwhile, make the dumplings. Sift the flour into a bowl, stir in the suet, parsley, and salt and pepper, then mix to a dough with the egg and water. About 15 minutes before the end of the cooking time, roll into small balls and drop into the simmering liquid.

Serve the meat on a hot dish surrounded by the vegetables and dumplings. Accompany by boiled potatoes and some of the cooking liquor in a gravy boat.

COOK'S NOTE
If boned and rolled brisket, or top breast as it is sometimes called, is used, it takes 4–5 hours to cook, but is also delicious.

Serves 6
Preparation time: 30 minutes
Cooking time: 2–2½ hours
Oven temperature: 425°F

oil, for frying

3½–4 lb. flank steak, tied into a neat shape

1 onion, stuck with 6 cloves

parsley, bay leaf, and celery stalk, tied together

1¼ cups stout

12–16 small pickling onions, peeled

1 lb. small carrots,

For the dumplings:

1 cup self-rising flour

2 oz. shredded suet

2 tablespoons finely chopped parsley

1 egg, beaten with 4 tablespoons cold water

salt and pepper

Irish Meat Loaf

¼ cup butter

1 oz. browned bread crumbs (see Cook's Notes)

1 small onion, finely chopped

1 lb. ground beef

4 oz. white bread crumbs

1 tablespoon tomato ketchup

1 teaspoon Worcestershire sauce

1 teaspoon crushed juniper berries

1 tablespoon finely chopped chives

1 tablespoon finely chopped parsley

1 teaspoon finely chopped oregano

1 egg, beaten

salt and pepper

Grease a 7½ x 3¾ x 2¼-inch loaf pan with half the butter and dust with the browned bread crumbs. Heat the remaining butter in a saucepan and fry the onion until soft, then add the beef and continue to cook until browning. Stir in the remaining ingredients and pack tightly into the prepared pan. Cover with foil and bake in a preheated oven for 1–1½ hours until firm to the touch. Allow to rest for 10–15 minutes before removing from the pan. Serve cut in slices, either hot or cold. A rich tomato sauce is a tasty accompaniment (see Cook's Notes).

COOK'S NOTES
To make browned bread crumbs, toast fresh white bread crumbs in the oven until dry and golden-brown.

This meat loaf mixture can also be used to make meat balls. Cook them in this delicious spicy tomato sauce made from 1 chopped onion and 1 chopped garlic clove, fried until soft. Add 14 oz. can plum tomatoes, ¼ cup plus 2 tablespoons stock, and a pinch each of sugar, basil, cinnamon, salt, and pepper, and simmer for 20 minutes.

Serves 4
Preparation time: 15–20 minutes
Cooking time: 1–1¼ hours
Oven temperature: 375°F

Oxtail Stew

Oxtail, although once widely used in the preparation of soups and stews, is less frequently used today. This particular stew, however, is rich and delicious and well worth remembering.

Heat the oil in a pan and fry the oxtail until well browned, then transfer to an ovenproof casserole dish. Fry the onion, also until brown, and add to the oxtail with the flour and tomato purée. Pour in the liquid and stir to blend. Add the carrots, thyme, bay leaf, mace, and season with salt and pepper. Bring to a boil. Cover, reduce the heat, and simmer very gently for 3–3½ hours until the meat is tender and falling off the bone. The stew can also be cooked in a preheated oven for the same length of time. Skim off excess fat, taste and adjust the seasoning, if necessary, and serve with mashed potatoes, champ, or jacket potatoes. Steamed celery hearts and broccoli are excellent accompaniments.

COOK'S NOTES
Oxtail stew is inclined to be quite fatty. For the best results, make the day before, refrigerate overnight, and just before use remove the fat which will have solidified on top.

Serves 4–6
Preparation time: 20–30 minutes
Cooking time: 3–3½ hours
Oven temperature, if using: 300–325°F

1 large oxtail, about 3 lbs., cut into 2-inch lengths

oil, for frying

1 large onion, sliced

½ cup flour

2 tablespoons tomato purée

6 cups beef stock, water, stout, or red wine

2 large carrots, sliced

1 sprig of thyme

1 bay leaf

pinch powdered mace

salt and pepper

But lest your kissing should be spoiled,

Your onions must be thoroughly boiled.

(JONATHAN SWIFT)

Irish Stew

One of Ireland's most famous dishes, traditionally made with mutton. Since mutton is rarely available now, lamb chops from the neck or shoulder, or stewing lamb baked off the bone, is used instead.

2 lbs. neck of lamb, cut into rings about ¾-inch thick

2 large onions, sliced

2 lbs. "floury" potatoes, sliced

2 large carrots, sliced

2–3 tablespoons finely chopped parsley

1¾ cups lamb stock or water

salt and pepper

Layer the meat and vegetables in a deep saucepan or flameproof casserole dish. Sprinkle half the parsley over, and season between each layer with salt and pepper; finish with a layer of potatoes. Pour in the stock or water and cover tightly with a piece of buttered waxed paper. Cover this with foil and a tightly fitting lid. Bring to a boil, then reduce the heat and simmer very gently for 1½–2 hours, either on top of the stove or in a preheated oven, until the meat is tender, the liquid well absorbed, and the stew rich and pulpy. If the potatoes are waxy in texture, they will not break down into the liquid. To thicken the juices, remove a few of these slices, mash them, and return to the pan. Add the remaining parsley, taste, and adjust the seasoning, if necessary. Serve with a glass of stout.

COOK'S NOTES

Broad shoulder chops or stewing lamb removed from the bone can also be used for Irish Stew. The carrots are not traditional, but they make a more tasty and interesting dish.

The cooking liquid could be half stock and half stout as an alternative; this is also not traditional!

Serves 4

Preparation time: 20 minutes
Cooking time: 1½–2½ hours
Oven temperature: 325°F

poultry & game

Poultry has always been an important food and source of income, even for the poorest families. A hen could be bought, bartered, or stolen and, once acquired, cost practically nothing to keep. The eggs could not only be eaten, but exchanged for other groceries when money was short. Today, "white" meat has become more desirable for the health-conscious, and poultry has never been more popular. Game, however, is still the choice for the more sophisticated palate and the rural hunter and his family.

Squab, Steak, and Mushroom Pie

½ cup flour

6 squab breasts, approximately 1½ lbs., cut into 1-inch cubes

1½ lbs. chuck steak, cut into 1-inch cubes

oil, for frying

1 large onion, finely chopped

10 oz. mushrooms, sliced

¾ cup plus 2 tablespoons stout

¾ cup plus 2 tablespoons beef or game stock

1 bay leaf and parsley sprigs

½ teaspoon allspice

1 tablespoon chopped parsley

salt and pepper

For the pastry:

1 lb. flaky or puff pastry

flour, for rolling

1 egg, beaten

Season the flour with salt and pepper and toss the squab and the steak in the flour. Fry in batches, in the hot oil, until brown. Transfer to a large casserole and add any remaining flour. Fry the onion and mushrooms until lightly browned and add to the meat. Pour in the stout and boil, scraping up any residue stuck to the pan. Add to the casserole with the remaining ingredients and season with salt and pepper. Bring to a boil, cover and simmer for about 1½ hours until the meat is tender. Allow to cool.

Remove the bay leaf and parsley stalks and put into a 1½ quart pie dish. Roll out the pastry on a floured surface and cover the squab and steak mixture, making a double crust around the pie dish rim, sealing well and fluting the edges. Decorate with the pastry trimmings, brush with beaten egg, and bake in a preheated oven for 20–25 minutes until risen and golden-brown. Serve hot.

COOK'S NOTES
Alternatively, the casserole can have a crumble topping. Cut ¼ cup butter into 1½ cups flour, add 1 tablespoon mixed fresh herbs, and 2 oz. grated hard cheese. Spread over the stew and bake in a preheated oven at 350°F for 20–25 minutes.

Serves 4–6
Preparation time: 45 minutes
Cooking time: about 2 hours, plus cooling time
Oven temperature: 425°F

Boned Stuffed Chicken

½ cup butter

1 large onion, finely chopped

8 oz. fine white bread crumbs

1 tablespoon finely chopped parsley

1 tablespoon finely chopped chervil

1 tablespoon finely chopped tarragon

1 egg, beaten

4–5 lb. roasting chicken, boned, with the skin unpunctured

2 large slices frying ham, cut ⅛-inch thick, rind removed

12 oz. pork sausage meat

1¼ cups hot chicken stock

salt and pepper

Melt half the butter in a pan and fry the onion until soft but not brown. Stir in the bread crumbs, herbs, and season with salt and pepper. Bind with the beaten egg. Allow to cool. To bone the chicken, see Cook's Notes.

Stuff the chicken. Pull the wings and legs through to the inside and flatten the flesh of the bird. Lay the two slices of ham over the breast meat, divide the sausage meat in half, and spread over the ham. Lay a log of the stuffing down the center from top to tail. Fold over the sides of the chicken, tucking in excess flesh and skin at the neck and tail. Don't stretch; otherwise the skin will burst. Stitch the edges together.

Set in a roasting pan, breast side up. Rub with the remaining butter, pour in the stock, and cook in a preheated oven for approximately 2 hours. Serve hot or cold, cut into about 20 slices.

COOK'S NOTES

To bone the chicken, cut off the ends of the legs and wings at the first joints and remove the wishbone. Place the bird breast side down on a board and cut along the backbone, working from the tail to the neck end. Scrape the flesh from the rib cage, working down one side of the bird until the wing is reached. Ease the knife between the ball and socket joint and sever from the rib cage, while keeping it attached to the skin. Continue easing away the flesh from the bone until you reach the leg joint. Sever the ball and socket joint. Continue in this way until you reach the breastbone. Turn the chicken and repeat the process on the other side of the bird. Separate the breastbone from the skin. Finally, lay the chicken flat on a board with the skin side down. Scrape the flesh from the wing bone and remove. Repeat the process with the other wing bone and with both the leg bones.

Serves approximately 12–15

Preparation time: 30–40 minutes, plus boning the chicken
Cooking time: about 2 hours
Oven temperature: 375°F

Traditional Pot Roast Chicken with Parsley Stuffing

Melt the butter in a pan and fry the onion until soft. Stir in the bread crumbs, chopped herbs, and season with salt and pepper. Bind with the beaten egg. Allow to cool.

Heat the oil in a pan and fry the bacon and pearl onions until brown. Transfer to a large pot or ovenproof casserole. Stuff the chicken breast and body cavity. To truss the chicken, see Cook's Notes.

Brown the trussed bird all over in the remaining fat. Set on top of the onions and bacon, and add the remaining ingredients. Bring to a boil, cover, and simmer until cooked. Transfer the chicken to a large serving dish, surround with the vegetables, and keep warm while making the sauce.

Blend a tablespoon of butter and flour together and gradually whisk into the boiling cooking liquid until it thickens. Season to taste, strain, and serve with the chicken.

COOK'S NOTES

Trussing keeps the stuffing in position and holds the bird together so that it will sit easily for carving. To truss a bird, set it breast up and pull back the legs. Push a threaded trussing needle through the bird at the joint of one knee. Turn the bird onto its breast, pull the neck skin over the neck cavity, and secure with a stitch which passes through both the wings. Next, turn the bird onto its side, pull the ends of the string from both the neck and the wing together, and fasten them firmly. Finally, turn the bird breast side up, tuck the tail into the body cavity, and tie the drumsticks together by stitching, in a figure of eight, under the breast bone and around the drumsticks.

Serves 4–6

Preparation time: 30 minutes, plus trussing
Cooking time: 1¼–1½ hours
Oven temperature: 350°F

¼ cup butter, plus extra for thickening the sauce

1 large onion, finely chopped

4–5 oz. fine white bread crumbs

3 tablespoons finely chopped parsley

pinch dried mixed herbs

1 small egg, beaten

2 tablespoons oil

½ lb. bacon, in a piece, cut into large cubes

12 pearl onions, peeled

3½–4½ lb. roasting chicken

1 lb. carrots, cut in chunks

8 oz. turnip, cut in chunks

1 bouquet garni (see Cook's Notes, page 19)

1½ cups strong chicken stock

flour, for thickening the sauce

salt and pepper

Chicken Frigasse

1½ lb. cooked boneless chicken breast, cut in large finger strips

6 oz. button mushrooms, fried

16 pickling onions, skinned and boiled

For the sauce:

¼ cup butter

½ cup flour

1¼ cups chicken stock

1¼ cups milk

1 egg yolk

¼ cup plus 1 tablespoon heavy cream

1–2 tablespoons Worcestershire sauce

1 tablespoon mustard

1 teaspoon anchovy paste

2 teaspoons capers

2 tablespoons finely chopped parsley

salt and pepper

For the garnish:

8 slices bacon, cut in half, rolled and broiled

4 lemon wedges

bunch of watercress

paprika

Make the sauce: melt the butter in a saucepan, stir in the flour, and gradually add the stock and milk until blended. Bring to a boil, stirring constantly until thickened and smooth, and cook for a few minutes. Mix the egg yolk and the cream together and whisk into the sauce with the remaining ingredients. Fold in the chicken pieces, stir in the mushrooms and onions, and heat thoroughly. Serve on a large flat dish garnished with the bacon rolls, lemon wedges, watercress, and a dusting of paprika.

COOK'S NOTES

Frigasse or fricassee is a word used to describe a method of preparing poultry, lamb, veal, rabbit, fish, and vegetables by boiling or stewing in stock or milk. This liquid is then thickened with egg yolk and cream and the meat or vegetables served in it.

Serves 4–6
Preparation time: 30 minutes
Cooking time: 15–30 minutes

Rabbit Frigasse

A rich stew of rabbit meat which was a particularly popular dish in large country houses in Ireland, during the eighteenth and nineteenth centuries.

To joint the rabbit, see Cook's Notes.

Cover the rabbit with water and a little salt and vinegar. Soak overnight to whiten and tenderize the flesh. Discard the soaking water, cover with fresh water, and bring to a boil. Discard this boiling water and simmer the rabbit in the stock, milk, onions, and herbs for 1–2 hours until tender. Reserve the cooking liquor.

Melt the butter in a pan, stir in the flour, and gradually add 2 cups of the cooking liquor. Bring to a boil, stirring constantly. Reduce the heat and simmer until smooth and thick. Stir in the cream and mustard, and season with salt and pepper. Add the rabbit pieces along with the fried mushrooms. Heat thoroughly, then serve, garnished with the parsley.

COOK'S NOTES
Rabbit bred for the table will take much less time to cook than wild rabbit.

To joint the rabbit, remove the ribs, shoulder, and neck, cutting from the body just below the ribs. Use to make stock. Divide the saddle and legs just above the top of the legs, remove the membrane and flap, cut the saddle and the legs in half.

Serves 4
Preparation time: 30 minutes, plus soaking the rabbit overnight
Cooking time: 1–2 hours

1–2 rabbits, to yield approximately 3½ lbs. when prepared

salt

vinegar

2½ cups chicken stock

1¼ cups milk

2 large onions, thinly sliced

bay leaf, sprig of thyme, and parsley sprigs tied together

For the sauce:

¼ cup butter

½ cup flour

½ cup cream

1 teaspoon mustard

salt and pepper

For the garnish:

6 oz. button mushrooms, fried in butter

2 tablespoons finely chopped parsley

Venison Stew with Parsnip and Potato Champ

1–2 tablespoons oil

1 onion, finely chopped

1½–2 lbs. lean venison, off the bone, cut into 1-inch cubes

¼ cup flour

1 cup stout

3 cups game stock or water

1 bay leaf

1 sprig marjoram

12–18 pickling onions, peeled

4–6 oz. celery, cut in 1-inch lengths

2 tablespoons finely chopped parsley

salt and pepper

Heat half the oil in a large skillet and fry the onion until soft and beginning to brown. Transfer to a large flameproof casserole. Heat the remaining oil in a pan and fry the meat, a little at a time, until brown. Mix with the onions. Stir in the flour and add the stout and stock, along with the bay leaf and marjoram, and season with salt and pepper. Bring to a boil, then reduce the heat and simmer gently for 1–1½ hours until the meat is almost tender. The stew can also be cooked in the oven for the same length of time. Add the pickling onions and celery 15–30 minutes before the end of the cooking time. Taste, and adjust the seasoning if necessary. Stir in the parsley and serve with parsnip champ (see Cook's Notes).

COOK'S NOTES
Allow 1 lb. potatoes and 1 lb. parsnips, washed and peeled, for 4 servings. Boil both separately until tender, drain, and dry well. Mash together with plenty of butter and salt and pepper.

Serves 4–6
Preparation time: 15 minutes
Cooking time: 1½–2 hours
Oven temperature: 300–325°F

Roast Heather Honey Duck with Walnut Stuffing

5–6 lb. dressed duckling

2 tablespoons lemon juice

2 tablespoons honey (use heather honey, if available)

2 tablespoons flour

1¼ cups duck or chicken stock

salt and pepper

For the stuffing:
1 tablespoon oil or rendered duck fat

1 onion, finely chopped

4 oz. walnuts, chopped

4 oz. fresh white bread crumbs

grated rind of 1 lemon

1 tablespoon chopped parsley

1 teaspoon marjoram, chopped

1 egg, beaten

Make the stuffing. Heat the oil in a pan and fry the onion until soft. Stir in the walnuts, bread crumbs, lemon rind, parsley, and marjoram, and season with salt and pepper. Bind with the egg.

Prick the duck all over with a fine skewer. Fill the body cavity with the stuffing. Truss the duck (see page 81) and set on a wire rack in a roasting pan. Mix the lemon juice and honey together and brush over the duck. Season with salt and pepper. Cook in a preheated oven for 10 minutes, then reduce the heat and cook for 25 minutes per pound, allowing 10–15 minutes resting time. Baste frequently during the cooking, brushing with any remaining lemon and honey mixture. Remove from the oven and drain off all but 1 tablespoon fat. Stir in the flour, blending with the cooking juices; add the stock and boil to thicken for the gravy.

Serve with Roasted Root Vegetables (see page 98) and boiled cabbage (see page 63).

COOK'S NOTES
When roasting any type of meat or poultry, it is important to allow 10–15 minutes resting time before carving to let the flesh relax. Carving straight from the oven can result in tough meat. Cover the meat and keep in a warm place while resting.

Serves 4
Preparation time: 20 minutes
Cooking time: 2–2½ hours
Oven temperature: 425°F for 10 minutes, then reduce the temperature to 375°F for the remainder of the cooking time.

Roast Goose with Apple and Whiskey Stuffing

12 lb. goose, oven-ready with giblets to make stock

1 Cox's apple, peeled, cored, and grated to yield approximately 5 oz.

2 tablespoons malt whiskey

2 tablespoons butter

1 onion, finely chopped

8 oz. coarse white bread crumbs

2 tablespoons finely chopped parsley

1 tablespoon finely chopped sage

pinch grated lemon rind

1 egg, beaten

salt and pepper

To truss the goose, see page 81. Prick the bird all over with a fork. Set on a wire rack in a roasting pan. Season with salt and pepper. Cook in the preheated oven for 20–25 minutes per pound. Pour off the fat several times during the cooking. Reserve for future use.

Soak the grated apple in the whiskey. Melt the butter in a pan and fry the onion until soft, then add the soaked apple, bread crumbs, herbs, lemon rind, and season with salt and pepper. Bind with the egg. Grease a 1 quart ovenproof soufflé dish with goose fat and fill with the stuffing. Cover with foil and cook with the goose for 45 minutes. Some of the stuffing can be used to fill the cavity of small Cox's apples, which can be baked for 30 minutes with the goose. Rest the goose for 15–20 minutes in a warm place before carving. Serve the goose with gravy, roast potatoes, and braised red cabbage.

COOK'S NOTES

In Ireland goose is traditionally served at Michaelmas (September 29) and Christmas, when it is said to bring prosperity for the coming year.

The reserved goose fat is excellent for roasting potatoes and parsnips and for greasing baking pans. It will keep in the refrigerator for several months. Use the goose giblets to make stock for the gravy.

Serves 6

Preparation time: 30 minutes
Cooking time: 4–5 hours
Oven temperature: 475°F for 30 minutes, then reduce the heat to 375°F for 3½–4½ hours.

Roast Pheasant

Use the pheasant giblets to make stock for the gravy. Melt half the butter in a pan, fry the giblets along with the onion, celery, and carrot until browned. Pour on the red wine and boil rapidly to reduce by half. Add 1½ cups water, the bay leaf, and peppercorns. Simmer while preparing and roasting the pheasant.

Smear the pheasant with the remaining butter, season with salt and pepper, set in a roasting dish, and cook in a preheated oven for 20–25 minutes per pound. Baste several times during the cooking. Once the bird is cooked, cover loosely and allow to rest for 10 minutes before carving.

Meanwhile, strain the stock and boil rapidly to reduce to a little less than 1 cup. Drain all but 1 tablespoon of fat from the roasting dish, add the flour, and stir well to mix with the sediment. Blend in the stock. Boil, strain, and keep warm.

Serve the pheasant garnished with watercress and accompanied by Brussels sprouts, Roasted Root Vegetables (see page 98), roast potatoes, and gravy.

COOK'S NOTES
Since pheasant is a lean meat with a fine skin, it is important to smear it well with butter or oil and to baste it several times while roasting to protect it from drying out during the cooking. It can also be covered with slices of fatty bacon.

Serves 2
Preparation time: 20 minutes
Cooking time: 35–45 minutes
Cooking temperature: 425°F

¼ cup butter

pheasant giblets (heart, gizzard, and neck), washed

1 small onion, peeled and quartered

1 celery stalk, chopped

1 small carrot, sliced

¼ cup plus 1 tablespoon red wine

1 bay leaf

6 peppercorns

1 plump oven-ready pheasant, approximately 1¾ lb. in weight

2 tablespoons flour

salt and pepper

watercress, to garnish

Breast of Pheasant with Savoy Cabbage and Mustard Sauce

4–6 tablespoons clarified butter (see Cook's Notes, page 42)

3¾–5 oz. pheasant breasts, skin and wing bones removed

salt and pepper

fresh herbs, to garnish

For the sauce:

1¼ cups game stock

1¼ cups red wine

2 tablespoons port

2–4 tablespoons Irish whole grain mustard

1¼ cups light cream

For serving:

14 oz. Savoy cabbage, shredded

¼ cup butter

Heat the butter in a large skillet and cook the pheasant breasts skin side down over gentle heat for 3–4 minutes. Turn and cook on the second side for a further 3–4 minutes. Remove from the heat, season with salt and pepper, and allow to rest for 3 minutes before serving.

Make the sauce by combining the stock, wine, and port in a saucepan and reducing by half. Stir in the mustard and cream and reduce until the sauce thickens and coats the back of a spoon. Season to taste with salt and pepper.

Cook the cabbage, drain, toss in the butter, and season. Divide among the 4 plates, piling it in the center. Carve each pheasant breast into 3 flat slices and arrange in a fan on top of the cabbage. Spoon a little sauce over each breast and garnish with a fresh herb sprig. Serve with Champ (see page 101).

COOK'S NOTES
Cooking times will vary depending on the thickness of the pheasant breast. When cooked, the flesh should feel firm but springy to the touch. When sliced, it should be only just cooked through.

Serves 4
Preparation time: 10 minutes
Cooking time: 6–8 minutes

The farmer's goose, who in the stubble,

Has fed without restraint or trouble,

Grown fat with corn and sitting still,

Can scarce get o'er the barn door sill.

(JONATHAN SWIFT)

vegetable
dishes

Although vegetables, both wild and cultivated, have been eaten since prehistoric times, their importance outside the monasteries, with the exception of the potato, has been secondary. Those that have been enjoyed are the easily grown vegetables such as turnips, carrots, parsnips, onions, cabbages, and leeks, not forgetting the potato—the ubiquitous vegetable of Ireland.

Irish Farmhouse Bake

One of the most modern Irish dishes, combining the best traditional ingredients: potatoes, bacon, cream, and cheese. This is a delicious and economical family dish.

¼ cup butter

8 slices smoked Canadian bacon, cut in strips

1 large onion, finely chopped

4 oz. mushrooms, sliced

6 potatoes, boiled

1 tablespoon chopped parsley

⅔ cup heavy cream

4 oz. farmhouse cheddar cheese, grated

salt and pepper

Melt half the butter in a pan and fry the bacon until cooked and beginning to brown. Remove from the pan and fry the onion and mushrooms until cooked and beginning to color. Cut the potatoes into wedges and arrange with the fried bacon, mushrooms, and onions in an oval 1 quart ovenproof dish. Season with salt and pepper and add the parsley. Pour in the cream and cover with the grated cheese. Bake in a preheated oven for 20–30 minutes until crisp and golden on top and very hot. Serve on its own or with broiled tomatoes.

COOK'S NOTES

A few wild mushrooms added to this dish make it very special.

Other vegetables such as sliced zucchini, cooked broccoli florets, or cauliflower can be used as alternatives to the mushrooms. Irish smoked cheese and bacon can also give variety and flavor.

Serves 4
Preparation time: 30 minutes
Cooking time: 20–30 minutes
Oven temperature: 350°F

Mixed Mushroom Frigasse

6 tablespoons butter

1 onion, finely chopped

1 clove garlic, crushed

1¼ lb. mushrooms of your choice, cleaned and sliced, if large

1 teaspoon finely chopped marjoram

1 tablespoon finely chopped parsley

⅔ cup red wine

1 egg yolk

1 teaspoon corn flour (available in health food stores)

2 tablespoons cream

salt and pepper

For serving:

8 slices bread

2 tablespoons finely chopped parsley

Melt ¼ cup of the butter in a large skillet and fry the onion and garlic until soft but not brown. Add the prepared mushrooms and continue to cook over gentle heat for about 10 minutes to draw out their juices. The mushrooms should stew rather than fry. Add the marjoram, parsley, and red wine, and season with salt and pepper. Bring to a boil.

Blend the egg yolk with the corn flour and cream and use to thicken the wine and mushroom juices. Keep warm.

Toast the bread and cut a circle from each slice using a 3½-inch cookie cutter. Lay the circles of hot toast overlapping on 4 individual plates and divide the frigasse among them, placing it on the bread. Sprinkle with parsley and serve immediately.

COOK'S NOTES

Any variety of cultivated or wild mushroom can be used for this dish or one type only, depending on taste and availability.

The frigasse is also delicious with finger strips of fried bacon stirred in just before serving. Smaller portions make an excellent appetizer.

Serves 4 as a main course or 8 as an appetizer
Preparation time: 15–20 minutes
Cooking time: 20–25 minutes

Savory Stuffed Potato Cakes

Heat the oil in a pan and fry the onion and bacon until beginning to brown. Add the mushrooms and continue to fry until they too begin to brown. Stir in the tomato and parsley and season with salt and pepper. Allow to cool.

Prepare the Potato Bread dough (see page 129), but roll out slightly thinner and cut into 16 circles using a 3-inch cookie cutter. Moisten the edges of half the circles with a little water. Divide the filling among these, leaving a small rim around the edge. Use the remaining circles to cover the filling, pressing the edges together to seal. Heat a skillet with a little oil or butter, add the potato cakes, and cook until brown on both sides and warmed through. This will take about 8–10 minutes. Serve with salad and pickled beets.

COOK'S NOTES

Any cooked vegetables can be used for the filling along with chopped cooked ham, smoked or poached salmon, or smoked mackerel. Sometimes I use all vegetables for the filling and serve fried or broiled bacon and tomatoes on the side.

Serves 4
Preparation time: 30 minutes
Cooking time: 8–10 minutes

1 tablespoon oil

1 small onion, finely chopped

4 slices bacon, diced

4 oz. mushrooms, finely chopped

1 tomato, finely chopped

1 tablespoon finely chopped parsley

2 quantities Potato Bread dough (see page 129)

oil or butter for frying

salt and pepper

Roasted Root Vegetables

1 lb. carrots, peeled

1 lb. parsnips, peeled

1 lb. turnips, peeled

1 tablespoon oil

2 tablespoons honey

Cut the vegetables into ½-inch cubes. Heat the oil in the pan and quickly fry the vegetables until just colored. Transfer to a roasting dish, drizzle the honey over, toss to coat evenly and roast in the preheated oven for 1–1¼ hours, until tender and well glazed. Toss frequently during the cooking to prevent the honey from burning.

Serve with roast meat, poultry, and game.

Serves 6

Preparation time: 15 minutes

Cooking time: 1–1¼ hours

Oven temperature: 400°F

Parsnip Cakes

One of my grandmother's favorite recipes, made from fresh parsnips grown in her cottage garden. The puréed flesh is mixed with flour and seasoning, dipped in egg and bread crumbs, and fried in hot oil or bacon fat.

Put the parsnips, flour, butter, mace, and nutmeg in a large bowl, season with salt and pepper, and beat well to combine. Divide into 4 pieces and mold each piece into a round flat cake, about 3½ inches in diameter and ½–¾ inch deep. Cut each cake in half.

Dip each cake into the beaten egg, toss in bread crumbs, pressing them well into the cakes to give an even coating. Fry in a little hot oil for 3–4 minutes on each side until cooked through and an even golden color. Drain on paper towels and serve as a main course or an accompanying vegetable. Parsnip Cakes are particularly good served with pork, ham, or roast beef, as well as fried sausages or bacon.

COOK'S NOTES
Any root vegetable suitable for mashing such as carrots, potatoes, and turnips, can be used for this recipe, either on their own or in combinations. A variety of spices and herbs can also be added. The cakes can be shaped into small logs or croquettes and deep-fried.

Makes 8 cakes
Preparation time: 20–30 minutes
Cooking time: 6–8 minutes

1 lb. parsnips, cooked and mashed

6 tablespoons flour

2 teaspoons butter, melted

pinch ground mace

pinch ground nutmeg

1 egg, beaten

4–6 oz. fresh bread crumbs

oil, for frying

salt and pepper

Fried Turnip & Bacon

1 large turnip, approximately 3½ lbs. in weight, peeled and cubed

2 tablespoons butter

8 slices bacon

salt and pepper

Boil the turnip in a little water until tender. Drain well, and mash with half the butter until smooth. Season well with salt and pepper. Heat the remaining butter in a pan and fry the bacon until cooked and beginning to crisp. Remove from the pan and keep warm. Toss the mashed turnip in the bacon fat. Serve with the slices of bacon, and boiled potatoes in their jackets.

COOK'S NOTES
This is very much a country dish, perhaps not the most elegant in appearance, but delicious in flavor. Fried sausages are sometimes used instead of the bacon.

Serves 4
Preparation time: 15 minutes
Cooking time: 20 minutes

There was an old woman,

Who lived in a lamp,

She had not room,

To beetle her champ.

(Traditional Rhyme)

Champ

Champ, also known as cally, poundies, and pandy, is one of the most famous ways of serving Ireland's best loved vegetable—the potato. Champ is this country's way of serving mashed potatoes.

Heat a pan of salted water and boil the potatoes in their skins until tender. Drain and dry over low heat covered with a paper towel. Peel and mash well.

While the potatoes are cooking, put the milk and chopped scallions into a saucepan, bring to a boil, and simmer for a few minutes. Gradually beat the milk and onion mixture into the mashed potatoes to form a soft, but not sloppy, mixture. Beat in half the butter and season with salt and pepper. Divide among 4 warm plates or bowls. Make a well in the center of each serving, cut the remaining butter into 4 pieces, and put one piece in each of the hollows. Serve immediately.

2 lbs. potatoes, unpeeled

⅔ cup milk

4–5 scallions, finely chopped

¼–½ cup butter

salt and pepper

COOK'S NOTES
Traditionally, champ would have been served as a main meal, with a glass of milk or buttermilk. Today, however, it is used to accompany meats such as boiled ham and broiled sausages. Parsley, young nettle tops, peas, and fava beans can be substituted for the scallions.

Serves 4
Preparation time: 5 minutes
Cooking time: 20–25 minutes

She up's with her beetle,

And broke the lamp,

And then she had room,

To beetle her champ.

(TRADITIONAL RHYME)

Colcannon

Similar to champ, but flavored, colored, and textured by the addition of cooked and shredded kale, a member of the cabbage family. Traditionally served at Halloween.

1 lb. kale or green cabbage, stalk or core removed, and finely shredded

1 lb. potatoes, unpeeled

6 scallions or chives, finely chopped

⅔ cup milk or cream

½ cup butter

salt and pepper

Heat a pan of salted water and boil the kale or cabbage in boiling water until very tender. This will take 10–20 minutes. At the same time, heat another pan of salted water and boil the potatoes until tender. Place the scallions and the milk or cream in a pan and simmer over low heat for about 5 minutes.

Drain the kale or cabbage and mash. Drain the potatoes, peel and mash well. Add the hot milk and scallions, beating well to give a soft fluffy texture. Beat in the kale or cabbage, season with salt and pepper, and add half the butter. The colcannon should be a speckled, green color. Heat through thoroughly before serving in individual dishes or bowls. Make a well in the center of each serving and put a pat of the remaining butter in each. Serve immediately.

Colcannon, like champ, can be served as a main dish with a glass of buttermilk, or as an accompanying vegetable.

COOK'S NOTES
Sometimes I blend the kale in a food processor along with the hot milk and scallions before adding to the potatoes. This produces an even texture and overall green color, and makes an interesting alternative.

Serves 4–6
Preparation time: 15 minutes
Cooking time: 20 minutes

Did you ever eat Colcannon,

When 'twas made with yellow cream?

(TRADITIONAL RHYME)

puddings &
desserts

Ireland has often been described as the land of milk and honey because of the variety and quality of her produce; milk, bread, and honey being available in abundance. These, together with eggs, formed the basis of many of Ireland's traditional puddings and desserts, such as custards, baked puddings, and molds. Wild and cultivated fruits of all varieties were also used and eaten, either on their own, with honey and cream, or made into fruit fools, jelly creams, and pastry pies.

Bramble Mousse

A favorite autumn dessert, made from plump wild blackberries, puréed and mixed with cream and egg whites, to make a rich, well-flavored mousse.

1 lb. prepared blackberries

⅓–½ cup granulated sugar

juice of 1 lemon

½ oz. powdered gelatin

⅔ cup heavy cream, lightly whipped

2 egg whites

For the garnish:

⅔ cup heavy cream, whipped

6–8 whole blackberries

Put the blackberries, sugar, and lemon juice into a saucepan and simmer gently for 10 minutes. Press through a strainer into a large mixing bowl. Put the gelatin and 4 tablespoons water in a small ovenproof bowl and soak for a few minutes. Set the bowl into a saucepan of hot water and stir the gelatin slowly to dissolve. Pour into the blackberry purée, whisking constantly. When the mixture begins to set, fold in the cream.

Whisk the egg whites until they hold their shape and then fold into the mousse mixture. Pour into 6–8 individual serving dishes and chill until set. Garnish each serving with a dollop of cream and a whole blackberry.

COOK'S NOTES
Gooseberries, rhubarb, black currants, and raspberries can each be used as an alternative to the blackberries, sweetening to taste. The fruit can be made into a purée, and frozen until required.

Serves 6–8
Preparation time: 30 minutes

Irish Whiskey Syllabub

rind and juice of 1 large
lemon

6 tablespoons clear honey

8 tablespoons Irish malt
whiskey

1¼ cups heavy cream,
chilled

grated nutmeg, to garnish

Put the lemon rind and juice, honey, and whiskey into a large
bowl and allow to stand for as long as possible to develop the
flavors. Gradually whisk in the cream until the mixture begins to
thicken. Spoon into wine glasses and chill until required.

If the syllabub is left for several hours, it will separate into a
thick cream on top and a clear liquid at the bottom. Whether
served immediately as a thick creamy concoction or after a few
hours as a two-layered delight, the syllabub should be garnished
with nutmeg and served with Shortbread Fingers (see page 134).

Serves 4–6
Preparation time: 15 minutes

Gooseberry & Elderflower Fool

2 lbs. green gooseberries,
stems and bottoms
removed

2–3 sprigs elderflowers
(optional)

¾ cup granulated sugar

1¼ cups heavy cream,
whipped until thick and
holding its shape

fresh elderflowers, to
garnish

Put the gooseberries, ⅔ cup water, and the elderflowers (if using)
into a saucepan and simmer gently until the fruit is soft. Remove
the elderflowers and pour the fruit into a strainer to drain the
excess juice. Put the fruit into a bowl and beat with a fork to form
a purée. Stir in enough sugar to sweeten.

Carefully fold the cream into the gooseberry purée to
combine. Spoon into 4 small glasses or dishes and chill well.
Garnish with elderflowers and serve with ladyfingers or
Shortbread Fingers (see page 134).

Serves 4–6
Preparation time: 20–30 minutes

Rich Shortcrust Pastry

*Halve the quantities of flour, butter, and lard and use
1 teaspoon granulated sugar, 1 egg yolk, and 2 teaspoons cold water
to make 4 oz. pastry, which will line an 8-inch tart pan.*

Sift the flour and salt into a large mixing bowl, then cut the butter
and lard into the flour and rub in until the mixture resembles fine
bread crumbs. Stir in the sugar. Mix the egg yolk with 3–4
tablespoons water and sprinkle over the top of the crumbled
mixture. Mix with a broad-bladed knife to form a stiff dough.
Work just long enough to form a ball. Allow the pastry to rest in
the refrigerator for about 30 minutes before using.

COOK'S NOTES
*The food processor is a most convenient way to make shortcrust
pastry and gives excellent results. Success, however, depends on
careful processing to ensure that the dough is not overworked.*

*Pastry freezes well and can therefore be prepared in
advance.*

Makes pastry for an 8-inch double-crust tart
Preparation time: 15 minutes
Cooking time: see individual recipes
Oven temperature: between 350°F to 400°F; see individual
recipes

2 cups flour

pinch salt

¼ cup butter or margarine

¼ cup lard

1 tablespoon granulated
sugar

1 egg yolk

Irish Apple Pie

For the filling:

3–3½ lbs. Bramley cooking apples, peeled, cored, and thinly sliced

5 tablespoons granulated sugar

6 whole cloves

granulated sugar, for sprinkling

For the pastry:

2½ cups flour

pinch salt

1 stick plus 2 tablespoons butter or margarine

¼ cup plus 2 tablespoons lard

1 tablespoon granulated sugar

1 egg yolk

4–5 tablespoons cold water

Prepare the pastry (see page 109). Divide into two pieces and roll one piece 1½ inches larger than an ovenproof pie plate. Line the plate with the pastry, cutting off the excess. Brush the pastry rim with lightly beaten egg white (reserved from making the pastry) and lay the pastry trimmings on top.

Arrange alternate layers of apples and sugar in the center of the plate with the cloves. Roll out the second piece of pastry just large enough to cover the pie. Brush the pastry rim with egg white and cover the pie with the pastry lid. Press the edges firmly together to seal and flute to decorate. Brush the pie with the remaining egg white and sprinkle with granulated sugar. Bake in a preheated oven for 10 minutes, then reduce the temperature and bake for a further 20–30 minutes, until the apples are just tender and the pastry is pale gold in color. Sprinkle with more granulated sugar and serve hot or cold with whipped cream.

COOK'S NOTES

For Rhubarb Tart, use 2–3 lbs. rhubarb, cut in ¾-inch lengths, tossed in 2 tablespoons corn flour (available in health food stores).

For Apple and Blackberry Pie, use 2 lbs. cooking apples and 1 lb. blackberries.

Serves 6–8

Preparation time: 30 minutes

Cooking time: 30–40 minutes

Oven temperature: 400°F for 10 minutes, then reduce the temperature to 350°F for a further 20–30 minutes

Treacle Tart

One of the many dessert dishes that found their way to Ireland via the Anglo-Irish and are now much enjoyed throughout the country.

4 oz. Rich Shortcrust Pastry (see page 109)

For the filling:

6 oz. fresh white bread crumbs

1¼ cups plus 1 tablespoon golden syrup, if available (see Cook's Notes)

grated rind of 1 lemon

¼ cup lemon juice

Roll out the pastry thinly on a floured surface and use to line an 8-inch fluted flan ring or springform tart pan, about 1½ inches deep. Mix the ingredients for the filling and pour into the pastry case. Bake in a preheated oven for 20–30 minutes until the pastry is cooked and golden. Serve hot or cold with lightly whipped cream.

Serves 6–8
Preparation time: 20–30 minutes
Cooking time: 20–30 minutes
Oven temperature: 375°F

COOK'S NOTES
Golden syrup is readily available in the United Kingdom but not in the U.S. An acceptable substitute is 1 part dark corn syrup and 5 parts light corn syrup.

Irish Coffee

Warm a stemmed whiskey glass or goblet with hot water. Put the sugar in the bottom of the glass and add very hot coffee to within 2 inches from the top of the glass. Stir to dissolve the sugar. Add the whiskey.

Hold a teaspoon, curved side up, across the glass, barely touching the coffee, and pour the cream very slowly over the spoon so that it floats on top of the coffee. The cream should be suspended on top of the whiskey-laced coffee (it hasn't worked if it falls to the bottom). Serve after a meal, as a pick-me-up, or as an excuse to celebrate.

Serves 1
Preparation time: 5 minutes

1 heaping teaspoon light brown sugar

1 cup of strong black coffee

approximately 1 double measure of Irish whiskey (4 tablespoons)

1–2 tablespoons chilled thick heavy cream

Irish Whiskey Trifle

Cut the jelly roll into ½-inch slices and arrange in a 1½ quart glass bowl. Sprinkle the whiskey over the cake slices and top with the raspberries, reserving a few for decoration. Allow to soak while preparing the custard.

Place the cream in a saucepan and gently bring to simmering point. Beat the egg yolks, granulated sugar, and corn flour together until pale in color. Pour in the cream, stirring constantly. Return the custard to the saucepan and cook over low heat until thick, stirring constantly. Cool slightly before pouring over the trifle.

When cool, spread the whipped cream on top of the custard and decorate with the remaining raspberries.

COOK'S NOTES
Trifle has many variations based on individual families' preferences. This basic trifle can be varied by using 1¼ cups custard made with custard powder instead of homemade custard and a can of mixed fruit instead of the raspberries. A fruit jelly can also be used to moisten the sponge and the fruit.

Serves 6–8
Preparation time: 30–40 minutes

1 lb. jelly roll, preferably homemade, filled with raspberry jam

¼ cup Irish whiskey

8 oz. frozen raspberries

1¼ cups heavy cream, whipped to hold its shape, to decorate

For the custard:

1¼ cups heavy cream

3 egg yolks

2 tablespoons granulated sugar

1 teaspoon corn flour (available in health food stores)

Irish Cheese Plate with Spiced Fruit Compote

1½ cups red wine

⅔ cup pure orange juice

grated rind and juice of 1 lemon

2-inch stick cinnamon

6 whole peppercorns

6 whole allspice berries

1 blade of mace

12 oz. mixed dried fruit (apricot, peaches, prunes, pears, dates, bananas, or figs)

For the cheese plate:

a selection of 5–8 Irish cheeses (see Cook's Notes). Allow approximately 3 oz. of cheese per person

watercress leaves, to garnish

Irish Oatcakes, to accompany (see page 126)

Combine the red wine, orange juice, water, lemon rind, and lemon juice in a large saucepan. Tie the spices in a piece of cheesecloth and add to the pan. Bring to a boil, add the fruit, and simmer gently for 30–40 minutes until the fruit is pulpy and tender. Allow to cool.

Cut the cheese into equal triangles and arrange on large individual plates. Spoon a little of the spiced compote on the side, garnish with watercress leaves, and serve with Irish Oatcakes (see page 126).

COOK'S NOTES
Irish Cheeses:
Cashel Blue: Semi-soft blue
Rathgore: Blue-veined goat cheese, similar to Roquefort
Milleens: Soft Camembert type
Cooleeney: Soft Camembert type

St. Tola: Goat cheese, log
Gubbeens: Semi-soft with unique flavor
Gubbeens: Semi-hard, smoked
Fivemiletown: Oak smoked
Gabriel: Gruyère type
Irish Desmond: Hard, close-textured
Lavistown: Semi-hard, Cheshire type
Ring: Irish farmhouse cheddar type

Serves 4
Preparation time: 20 minutes
Cooking time: 30–40 minutes for the compote

Brown Bread & Irish Whiskey Ice Cream

Combine the bread crumbs and light brown sugar in a mixing bowl. Spread over a large baking sheet and bake in a preheated oven until the sugar has caramelized. This will take about 10 minutes. Allow to cool.

Whisk the eggs and granulated sugar until very thick and pale cream in color. Fold the caramelized bread into the eggs, followed by the whiskey and heavy cream. Whisk until it is just holding its shape. Pour into a strong container and freeze overnight.

Serve two scoops of ice cream per person. Decorate with a mint leaf and accompany with Shortbread Fingers (see page 134).

COOK'S NOTES

Irish wheaten bread is not suitable for this ice cream as it makes it rather heavy and unappetizing. However, any type of brown bread is excellent.

Freezing is done in the freezer with no stirring or churning required. An ice-cream maker is not needed.

Serves 9–10
Preparation time: 30 minutes, plus freezing overnight
Cooking time: 10 minutes, for the crumbs
Oven temperature: 475°F

6 oz. brown bread crumbs (not wheaten)

½ cup light brown sugar

3 eggs

¼ cup plus 1 tablespoon granulated sugar

⅓ cup Irish whiskey

1½ cups heavy cream

fresh mint leaves, to decorate

I'll have none of your boxty,

I'll have none of your blarney,

But I'll whirl my petticoats over my head

And be off with my Royal Charlie.

(Traditional Rhyme)

St. Brendan's Cream

½ cup St. Brendan's or
Bailey's Irish Cream
liqueur

¼ cup sweet white wine

2 tablespoons lemon juice

¼ cup granulated sugar

1¼ cups heavy cream

thin slices of lemon, to
garnish

Combine the liqueur, wine, lemon juice, and sugar in a bowl and
beat with an electric mixer to dissolve the sugar. Gradually add
the cream, beating constantly until the liquid begins to thicken.
The mixture will look slightly curdled at first but will improve in
texture as the mixing continues. When the mixture is holding its
shape, spoon into long-stemmed glasses. Chill for several hours to
develop the flavors before serving. Garnish with lemon slices.

Serves 6
Preparation time: 15 minutes

Carrageen Moss Blancmange

1½ oz. dried carrageen
moss

finely grated rind of
1 lemon

3¾ cups milk

1 egg, separated

2–3 tablespoons
granulated sugar

Put the carrageen moss, lemon rind, and milk into a pan and
slowly bring to a boil. Simmer gently for 15–20 minutes until
the carrageen swells and exudes jelly. Whisk the egg yolk and
granulated sugar together until pale in color, and pour on the
carrageen mixture, rubbing all the jelly through a strainer. Stir
to combine. Return to a clean pan, bring to a boil, and cook
over gentle heat until the mixture coats the back of a wooden
spoon. Allow to cool. Whisk the egg white until stiff and gently
fold into the cold carrageen mixture. Pour into a 1 quart
dampened mold or six ½-cup individual molds or dishes.
Refrigerate until set. Turn out of the mold and serve chilled
with lightly stewed fruit or fresh berries.

COOK'S NOTES
*Carrageen is an edible seaweed also known as "Irish Moss" or
"Sea Moss." It is a rich source of agar jelly and is used for
thickening both sweet and savory dishes.*

Serves 4–6
Preparation time: 10 minutes, plus cooling and setting

Bramley Apple Cheesecake

Stir the melted butter into the cracker crumbs, press into the bottom of a lightly greased 8-inch springform pan about 2 inches deep.

Stew the apples with the lemon juice and 1 tablespoon of water until soft. Stir in the sugar and egg yolks and allow to cool. Add the cheese and blend in a blender until smooth. Pour into a large bowl. Dissolve the gelatin in 3 tablespoons of water and add to the apple mixture. Lightly whisk the egg whites and fold into the apple mixture with the cream and pour into the pan. Refrigerate overnight until set. Remove from the pan and decorate with dollops of cream and apple slices.

COOK'S NOTES

This cheesecake is also excellent made with ricotta cheese. Soaking the apple slices in a little lemon juice for the garnish prevents them from discoloring.

Serves 8–10

Preparation time: 30 minutes, plus overnight refrigeration

¼ cup unsalted butter, melted

⅔ cup Graham crackers, crushed

For the filling:

2 lbs. Bramley apples, peeled, cored, and sliced

1 tablespoon lemon juice

¼ cup plus 2 tablespoons granulated sugar

2 eggs, separated

8 oz. cream cheese

½ oz. powdered gelatin

1 cup heavy cream, lightly whipped

For the garnish:

⅔ cup heavy cream, whipped

red-skinned apple, thinly sliced

Irish Curd Cheesecake

This is an eighteenth century dessert, adapted from the recipe manuscript of Lady Rivers, County Cavan, 1750.

4 oz. Rich Shortcrust Pastry (see page 109)

confectioners' sugar, for dusting

For the filling:

¼ cup butter, softened

¼ cup granulated sugar

rind of 1 large lemon

juice of ½ lemon

pinch ground cinnamon

3 eggs, separated

3 tablespoons flour

12 oz. cottage cheese, strained

For the topping:

1 egg

1 tablespoon granulated sugar

2 tablespoons butter, melted

1 tablespoon flour

Roll out the pastry until about ⅛-inch thick and use to line an 8-inch springform pan. Set the pan on a baking sheet.

Cream the butter and sugar together until light and fluffy, then beat in the lemon rind and juice, cinnamon, egg yolks, and flour. Beat the egg whites until stiff and fold into the mixture. Pour into the pastry shell.

Combine all the ingredients for the topping and pour on top of the filling. Bake in a preheated oven for 1–1¼ hours until the cake is golden, risen, and firm to the touch. Allow to cool in the pan before removing. Sprinkle with confectioners' sugar and serve with cream or natural yogurt.

COOK'S NOTES

This was a very popular cake and dessert in Ireland during the eighteenth century, often flavored with sherry, a favorite drink of the time. Sometimes, rose water would also have been used and the filling varied by the addition of 2–4 oz. dried fruit.

Serves 6–8

Preparation time: 30 minutes
Cooking time: 1–1¼ hours
Oven temperature: 325°F

breads & cakes

The making of bread in its many different forms is one of the great traditions of the Irish kitchen. Bread is made with both bleached and whole wheat flour, flavored with treacle and fruit, and raised with buttermilk—the milk that is left over after the butter is removed from the churn. These breads, lovingly referred to as white and brown soda, are baked either on the griddle, or in the oven. Although bread is the cornerstone of the Irish baking tradition, the country is equally well-known for its cakes of all shapes and sizes, along with its cookies, tarts, and sweets.

Currant Soda

4 cups soda bread flour
(see Cook's Notes, p. 125)

1 heaping teaspoon baking
soda

pinch salt

¼ cup granulated sugar

4 oz. dried fruit

1¾–2 cups buttermilk

1 tablespoon butter

Sift the flour and baking soda into a large mixing bowl, then stir in the salt, sugar, and fruit. Make a well in the center and pour in almost all of the buttermilk. Stir with a broad-bladed knife or wooden spoon to form a loose dough, adding the rest of the milk if necessary.

Use the butter to grease an 8-inch round cake pan, approximately 3 inches deep. Place the dough in the pan, leaving the surface rough. Sprinkle with a little flour, set the pan on a baking sheet, and bake in a preheated oven for 30 minutes. Reduce the temperature and cook for a further 30 minutes until the bread is golden-brown and crisp to the touch. A skewer inserted in the center should come out clean. Remove from the cake pan and wrap in a clean cloth. When cool, cut in slices and serve buttered.

COOK'S NOTES
A savory soda bannock can be made by adding cooked, chopped bacon, ham, and herbs instead of the fruit, along with a strongly flavored cheddar cheese.

Makes 1 round loaf
Preparation time: 10–15 minutes
Cooking time: 1–1¼ hours
Oven temperature: 400°F for 30 minutes, then reduce the temperature to 300°F for a further 30–40 minutes

Soda Farls

2½ cups soda bread flour
1 teaspoon salt
1–1¼ cup buttermilk
extra flour, for dusting

Sift the flour and salt into a large bowl. If using all-purpose flour and baking soda and cream of tartar (see Cook's Notes), sift with the flour. Make a well in the center and add nearly all of the buttermilk. Stir with a broad-bladed knife or wooden spoon to form a firm dough, adding the remaining milk if necessary.

Turn onto a lightly floured surface and knead lightly until a smooth ball is formed. Roll or pat out to form a circle approximately 8½ inches in diameter and no more than ½-inch thick. Cut into 4 farls or triangles.

Gently heat a griddle, heavy cast-iron pan or electric skillet, and sprinkle with a dusting of flour. When this begins to turn pale beige, the temperature is correct for cooking. Set the farls on the pan and cook for about 6–10 minutes on each side until risen and pale beige. When cooked, they will sound hollow when tapped.

Remove from the pan, wrap in a clean cloth until cool, and cut in half, butter generously, and eat immediately.

COOK'S NOTES

If soda bread flour is not available, use all-purpose flour plus ½ teaspoon of baking soda and ½ teaspoon of cream of tartar. Soda farls are an important feature of an Ulster Fry (see page 58) or as the container for holding a fried egg, bacon, sausage, and potato bread for a quick, but substantial, snack called a "sausage soda."

Makes 4 farls
Preparation time: 10–15 minutes
Cooking time: 12–20 minutes

White Soda Bread

Sift the flour, salt, and baking soda into a large mixing bowl and add the sugar. Make a well in the center and pour in almost all of the buttermilk, stirring with a broad-bladed knife or wooden spoon to mix to a spongy dough.

Use the butter to grease a 7½ x 4½ x 2½-inch loaf pan and pour the porridge-like mixture into this, spreading it in the pan, but leaving the surface rough. Sprinkle with a dusting of flour, place on a baking sheet, and bake in a preheated oven for 30 minutes. Reduce the oven temperature and cook for a further 30 minutes until the bread is well risen, light beige, and crusty on top. Remove from the oven, and cover with a cloth. After 5 minutes, remove from the pan, wrap in the cloth, and allow to cool before cutting. Serve cut in slices and buttered.

COOK'S NOTES

If soda bread flour is not available, use all-purpose flour plus 1 heaping teaspoon baking soda and 1 heaping teaspoon of cream of tartar.

All "soda" style Irish breads need to be eaten the day they are baked, and toasted or fried the second day.

Makes 1 x 1 kg/2 lb loaf
Preparation time: 10 minutes
Cooking time: 1 hour
Oven temperature: 400°F for 30 minutes, then reduce the temperature to 300°F for a further 30 minutes

4 cups soda bread flour

1 teaspoon salt

1 teaspoon baking soda

2 tablespoons–¼ cup granulated sugar

1¾–2 cups buttermilk

2 tablespoons butter

Irish Oatcakes

In Ireland, oats have always been an important and widely used food for making porridge and soup, coating fish, and baking bread and biscuits. These simple, flat cakes would originally have been baked on a griddle, over a turf fire, or on a warmed hearthstone.

8 oz. oatmeal

½ cup flour

½ teaspoon baking soda

¼ teaspoon cream of tartar

½ teaspoon salt

¼ cup butter

extra oatmeal, for shaping

Put the oatmeal in a large bowl and sift in the flour, baking soda, cream of tartar, and salt. Make a well in the center. Put ¼ cup hot water and the butter into a saucepan and bring to a boil. Pour into the well and mix to bind. Place on a work surface lightly scattered with oatmeal, and roll into a round cake about 9 inches in diameter and ⅛-inch thick. Scatter more oatmeal on top of the cake and press it into the surface. Cut into 8 triangular cakes. Place on a floured baking sheet and bake in a preheated oven for about 40 minutes.

COOK'S NOTES
These traditional oat biscuits are delicious with butter, cheese, and a glass of buttermilk.

They can also be cut into 3-inch rounds and served as circular biscuits.

Makes 8 triangular cakes
Preparation time: 15 minutes
Cooking time: 40 minutes
Oven temperature: 350°F

Griddle Scones

Combine the flour, sugar, and fruit in a large mixing bowl. Make a well in the center and pour in almost all of the buttermilk. Stir with a wooden spoon or broad-bladed knife to form a firm dough, adding the remaining milk if necessary.

Turn the dough onto a lightly floured surface and knead very gently until a smooth ball is formed. Pat to a circle about 8 inches in diameter and about ¼-inch thick. Cut into 6 triangular shapes.

Gently heat a cast-iron griddle or heavy-bottomed skillet and sprinkle with a little flour. When this begins to turn a pale beige, the temperature is correct for cooking. Place the scones in the pan and cook for 6–8 minutes on each side until risen and pale golden. Serve hot or cold with butter and jam.

COOK'S NOTES
The scones can be made without the fruit and salt, and savory items such as fried chopped bacon, ham, or herbs can be added for variety.

Makes 6 triangular scones
Preparation time: 10–15 minutes
Cooking time: 6–8 minutes

1¼ cups soda bread flour (see Cook's Notes, page 125)

1 teaspoon granulated sugar

1 oz. dried mixed fruit

½ cup–½ cup plus 2 tablespoons buttermilk

extra flour, for dusting

Irish Wheaten Bread

This particular bread is sometimes referred to as brown soda.

1½ cups soda bread flour

1 teaspoon baking soda

3 cups whole wheat flour

pinch salt

1–2 teaspoons brown sugar

1¾–2 cups buttermilk

1 tablespoon butter

Sift the soda bread flour and baking soda into a large mixing bowl. Add the whole wheat flour, salt, and sugar, stirring to blend. Make a well in the center and pour in almost all of the buttermilk, stirring with a broad-bladed knife or wooden spoon to form a loose dough.

Use the butter to grease a 7½ x 4½ x 2½ inch loaf pan. Place the dough into the pan, leaving the surface rough. Sprinkle with a little extra whole wheat flour to give a nutty surface. Place on a baking sheet and bake in a preheated oven for 30 minutes. Reduce the temperature and continue to cook for a further 30 minutes until the bread is well-risen, brown, and crusty on top. When a skewer inserted into the center comes out clean, the bread is done. Remove from the pan and wrap in a clean cloth. Place on a wire rack to cool. Serve cut in slices and buttered.

COOK'S NOTES

Traditionally, good-sized breakfast cups would be used for measuring, with 1 cup of all-purpose or soda bread flour being used to 2 cups of whole wheat flour and 1 cup of buttermilk.

The secret of good Irish bread is to mix quickly and lightly and not to overwork.

The texture of this bread can be varied depending on the coarseness of the whole wheat flour used.

Makes 2 lb. loaf

Preparation time: 10 minutes

Cooking time: 1 hour

Oven temperature: 400°F for 30 minutes, then reduce the temperature to 300°F for a further 30 minutes

Potato Bread

Put the potatoes into a large bowl and mix in the salt and butter. Stir in the flour to make a pliable dough. Place on a lightly floured surface and roll into a circular shape about ¼-inch thick and 9 inches in diameter. Cut into 6 farls (triangular shapes).

Potato bread is cooked on a cast-iron griddle or in a heavy-bottomed skillet which is heated gently with a light dusting of flour, without fat or oil. When this begins to turn a pale beige, the temperature is right for cooking. Arrange the farls in the pan and cook for about 2½ minutes on each side until lightly browned. Serve hot with butter and sugar or homemade jam. Alternatively, the baked bread may be fried and eaten with bacon, sausages, and egg as part of an Ulster Fry (see page 58).

COOK'S NOTES
Potato bread is best made while the potatoes are still hot. If using leftovers, heat for 30 seconds in the microwave before mixing with the rest of the ingredients.

The potato bread can also be cut into 10 circles with a 3-inch cookie cutter.

Makes 6 farls
Preparation time: 5 minutes
Cooking time: 5 minutes

8 oz. warm potatoes, cooked and mashed

½ teaspoon salt

2 tablespoons butter, melted

½ cup flour, plus extra for dusting

Boxty Pancakes

A traditional potato dish, found in the northern counties of Cavan, Donegal, Leitrim, and Monaghan. Boxty pancakes are sometimes referred to as stamp.

1 lb. potatoes, washed and peeled

2 tablespoons flour

1 teaspoon baking powder

salt and pepper

⅔ cup milk

oil, for frying

Grate the potatoes on a coarse grater into a bowl; add the flour, sifted with the baking powder. Season with salt and pepper and mix in the milk. Drop tablespoons of this mixture onto a hot, lightly oiled pan or griddle. Cook for about 5 minutes on each side until golden-brown. Serve hot with butter and sugar or fried bacon.

Makes 11 pancakes
Preparation time: 15 minutes
Cooking time: 30 minutes

Boxty on the griddle,

Boxty in the pan,

If you don't eat your boxty,

You'll never get a man.

Boxty on the griddle,

Boxty in the pan,

The wee one in the middle,

That one's for Mary Anne.

(TRADITIONAL RHYME)

Potato Apple Cake

This dish is the highlight of the farmhouse tea table during the apple season, and is also prominent in Halloween festivities, when it is traditional for a ring to be hidden in the filling, to bring luck.

8 oz. warm potatoes, cooked and mashed

½ teaspoon salt

2 tablespoons butter

½ cup flour

granulated sugar, to sweeten

¼ cup butter, to finish

For the filling:

10 oz. Bramley apples, peeled, cored, and very thinly sliced

Prepare the Potato Bread dough (see page 129). Divide this in two and roll each piece into an 8-inch circle. Divide the sliced apples between each circle, placing them on one half only. Moisten the edge of the circle with a little water and fold the uncovered half of the potato bread on top of the apples to form a half-moon shape. Press the edges together to seal.

Bake on a preheated griddle or pan for 15–20 minutes on each side to cook the apples and brown the bread. Just before serving, remove the cakes from the pan and set on a serving plate. Carefully open the cake along the curved edges, fold back the bread, sprinkle the apples with sugar, and dot with butter. Seal the edges once more and put the cakes in a hot oven for 5–10 minutes to form a thick syrup. Serve immediately.

COOK'S NOTES
The Potato Apple Cake can also be eaten cold, in which case, a little sugar is added to the apples before cooking and the outside of the cake buttered before serving.

Makes 2 large cakes
Preparation time: 15 minutes
Cooking time: 45–50 minutes

Sponge Cake with Raspberry Jam and Fresh Cream

Grease two 6-inch pans and dust with a mixture of flour and granulated sugar. Put the eggs and sugar in a large ovenproof bowl. Set this over a pan of hot water and whisk until light and creamy. The mixture should be stiff enough to retain the impression of the whisk for a few seconds. This will take about 5–8 minutes. Remove from the heat and whisk until cool.

Sift the flour and baking powder together and very lightly fold into the whisked mixture, one third at a time. Divide this between the two 6-inch pans and bake near the top of the oven for 20 minutes. Leave in the pans until cool.

Sandwich the cakes together with the jam and cream and dust with sifted confectioners' sugar.

COOK'S NOTES
For speed and convenience the eggs and sugar can be beaten in an electric mixer until thick and creamy. For an 8-inch cake use two 8-inch pans, 4 eggs, and cook for an extra 15 minutes.

Makes 6-inch sponge cake
Preparation time: 15 minutes
Cooking time: 20 minutes
Oven temperature: 350°F

3 eggs

½ cup granulated sugar

¾ cup flour

¼ teaspoon baking powder

3–4 tablespoons raspberry jam

⅔ cup heavy cream, whipped

confectioners' sugar, to dust

Shortbread Fingers

These short, buttery cookies are of Scottish origin and have been a feature of the Irish tea table for many years.

1 cup butter

¼ cup granulated sugar

½ cup corn flour (available in health food stores)

2½ cups flour

granulated sugar, for sprinkling

Cream the butter and sugar together until light and fluffy. Sift in the corn flour and all-purpose flour and mix well to combine. Press into an oblong pan approximately 12 x 8 inches and mark with the prongs of a fork in both directions. Bake in a preheated oven for 30 minutes. Reduce the temperature and cook for a further 1–1½ hours.

Remove from the oven and cut into 32 even-sized fingers. Sprinkle with granulated sugar and allow to cool slightly in the pan. Transferring to a cooling rack until firm. Store in an airtight container.

COOK'S NOTES
The length of the cooking time will depend on how pale or dark you prefer the cookies. Alternatively, this mixture can be rolled out thinly and cut into circular cookies. A little semolina can be added to give a more crunchy texture.

Makes 32 fingers
Preparation time: 15 minutes
Cooking time: 1½–2 hours
Oven temperature: 275°F for 30 minutes, then reduce the temperature to 250°F for 1–1½ hours

Tea Brack

The word "brack," or "breac," means speckled and refers to the fruit used in the dough. There are a number of different types of brack. This particular recipe is a cake rather than a bread and is moistened with tea.

9 oz. white raisins

9 oz. raisins

1 cup dark-brown sugar

2 cups strong black hot tea

1 tablespoon butter, melted

3 cups flour

2 teaspoons baking powder

2 teaspoons mixed spice

2 eggs, beaten

Put the fruit and sugar into a large bowl and pour in the hot tea. Stir to dissolve the sugar, cover, and leave overnight to allow the fruit to swell.

Line the bottom and sides of an 8 x 3-inch round cake pan with waxed paper and grease lightly with the melted butter.

Sift the flour, baking powder, and spice together and mix into the fruit mixture alternately with the eggs, beating well between each addition. Pour into the prepared pan, smooth the top, and bake in a preheated oven for approximately 1½ hours. Allow to cool in the pan before turning out onto a wire rack. When cool. store in an airtight container.

Makes 8 x 3-inch round cake
Preparation time: 15 minutes, plus overnight soaking
Cooking time: about 1½ hours
Oven temperature: 325°F

Dropped Scones

Put the flour into a large mixing bowl with the sugar. Make a well in the center, break in the egg, and beat with a wooden spoon to make a thick batter, gradually adding the buttermilk. Draw the flour from the sides of the bowl to the center to prevent lumps from forming.

Slowly heat a cast-iron griddle or heavy-bottomed skillet over gentle heat. Grease lightly with a pat of butter, wiping most of it off with a paper towel. Drop the batter from the point of a tablespoon into the pan. The scones will immediately begin to rise. When a few bubbles begin to break on the surface, the scones are ready for turning. Turn them over gently and brown on the other side. When the scones are cooked, they should be golden-brown, and light and spongy in texture. Keep warm in a clean tea towel until they are all cooked. Serve with butter and jam.

COOK'S NOTES

If soda bread flour is not available, use 1 cup flour with 1 teaspoon baking soda and 1 teaspoon cream of tartar.

These little dropped scones are traditionally served hot for afternoon tea.

Makes 14 scones

Preparation time: 5 minutes
Cooking time: 15 minutes

1 cup soda bread flour

2 tablespoons granulated sugar

1 egg

⅔ cup buttermilk

2 teaspoons butter, for greasing

Buttermilk Scones

2 cups flour, plus extra for dusting

1 teaspoon baking soda

1 teaspoon cream of tartar

pinch of salt

2 tablespoons butter

¾ cup plus 2 tablespoons buttermilk

beaten egg or milk, to glaze (optional)

Sift the dry ingredients into a bowl. Cut the butter into small pieces and rub into the flour until the mixture resembles fine bread crumbs. Make a well in the center and add almost all of the buttermilk, mixing with a wooden spoon or broad-bladed knife to form a soft dough. Place on a lightly floured surface and knead very gently to form a round shape. Roll out to about ¾-inch thick. Cut into scones using a 2–2½-inch cookie cutter.

Place on a lightly floured baking sheet and brush with egg or milk to glaze. Bake in a preheated oven for 15–20 minutes until well risen and light-golden. Serve hot or cold with butter or jam.

COOK'S NOTES
For fruit scones add 1–2 oz. dried fruit or cherries and ⅛–¼ cup granulated sugar before adding the milk.

For savory scones add 2 oz. grated cheese, some diced, cooked bacon, or herbs.

For wheaten scones, use half whole wheat flour and half all-purpose flour.

Makes 8–12 scones
Preparation time: 15 minutes
Cooking time: 15–20 minutes
Oven temperature: 425°F

Boiled Fruit Cake

Fruit breads and cakes are an important feature of the Irish tea table. This boiled cake is richly flavored with fruit and spice, and is more economical than a more traditional rich fruit cake.

Put the butter, sugar, fruit, and 1 cup water into a large saucepan. Bring to a boil, reduce the temperature and simmer for 10 minutes. Allow to cool. Sift the flour, baking powder, baking soda, and spice together and fold into the fruit mixture, along with the almond extract and beaten eggs.

Pour into a 7-inch deep cake pan, lined with waxed paper and well-greased. Bake in a preheated oven for 1½ hours until risen and set. Allow to cool slightly in the pan. Remove from the pan and allow to cool completely. Wrap in waxed paper or foil and store in an airtight container.

COOK'S NOTES
This cake is deliciously moist and perfect for afternoon tea. Serve in slices, spread with butter.

The cake will always taste better if the pan has been greased with melted butter.

Makes 7-inch cake
Preparation time: 20–30 minutes
Cooking time: 1½ hours
Oven temperature: 300°F

½ cup plus 2 tablespoons butter

½ cup plus 2 tablespoons brown sugar

12 oz. dried mixed fruit

2 cups flour

1 teaspoon baking powder

1 teaspoon baking soda

2 teaspoons mixed spice

½ teaspoon almond extract

2 eggs, beaten

glossary

Bacon: the sides of the pig, known as the "flitch," were cured as bacon. To cure the pig, the flesh was rubbed with a mixture of salt, sugar, and saltpeter, up to two weeks before being dried. It was often hung by the fire to smoke over a mixture of turf and oak. Today, most pork is cured in a salt solution.

Bairm Brack: the traditional bread eaten at Halloween. The word "breac" means speckled and refers to the fruit used in the dough. Bairm, which is yeast, was used to leaven the cake or bread. It is sometimes referred to as "barm" or "barn brack." When eaten at Halloween, the bread has "rings" hidden in the dough, which signifies marriage before Easter for whoever is lucky enough to find one in his or her slice. Bairm Brack is also popular throughout the year as a tea-time cake.

Baking Soda: also known as bicarbonate of soda or sodium bicarbonate. Used as a rising agent in Irish breads, along with "sour" milk.

Bannock: one of Ireland's most popular soda breads. The basic soda bread recipe is enriched with fruit. Traditionally cooked in a pot-oven, over a turf fire in the open hearth. It is served, cut in slices, with butter. Also known as fruit soda, currant soda, and curranty cake.

Bard: a poet or singer.

Beastlings: the first new milk given by a newly calved cow.

Black Pudding: also known as blood pudding. Made from cow, sheep or pig blood, mixed with fat, milk, or cream and cereal—generally oatmeal—herbs, spices, and seasoning. In appearance, black puddings resemble very plump sausages.

Brigid (Brigit): the daughter of Dagda and the goddess of healing, smiths, fertility, and poetry. Her festival, held on February 1, was one of the four great festivals of the Celtic world. (see also St. Brigid)

Broth: a substantial soup, flavored with meat, enriched with pulses and root vegetables, and thickened with cereal. The earliest broth was thickened with oats, giving it a porridge-like texture. Today, barley is more frequently used.

Brown Soda: soda bread made using whole wheat flour. (see also Soda Bread; Soda Bread Flour; White Soda)

Buttermilk: the milk left over after cream has been churned into butter. One of the main ingredients used in the making of traditional Irish breads. Also highly prized as a drink and at one time in country areas, served with almost every meal.

Buttermilk Plant: a plant-like structure composed of yeast and bacteria.

Byre: a cattle barn.

Carrageen: also known as sea moss and Irish moss. A branching, viscous seaweed found on coastal rocks all over Ireland. A rich source of agar jelly, which is used for thickening and setting sweet and savory dishes. It is sold dried in health food and specialty shops.

Cúchulainn: one of the most famous heroes of Irish mythology and reputedly the son of the god Lugh.

Curds: the by-product formed when milk is soured either naturally or by the addition of buttermilk or rennet. One of the most important foods for the Irish until the introduction of the potato in the seventeenth century. Eaten as they were or made into cheese.

Drisheen: the black pudding of county Cork. Made from sheep blood and flavored with the herb tansy, its texture resembles that of a baked custard.

Druids: ministers of the Celtic religion, as well as philosophers, advisers, judges, and teachers. Known throughout the Celtic world, not just in Ireland. In Irish mythology, they featured mainly as masters of the supernatural arts and were both male and female.

Fadge: another name for potato bread, or potato cake, most commonly used in the the northern counties of Ireland.

Frigasse: also known as frigacy or fricassee. Frigasse was the word used in a number of eighteenth century Irish manuscript "receipt" books to describe a method of preparing poultry or game. The meat is cut into pieces, cooked by stewing or boiling, served in a rich sauce made from the cooking liquor, thickened with egg yolk and cream.

Gael: the son of Niul, the progenitor of the Gaelic people.

Ham: the hind legs of the pig, a prime cut, dry or wet, cured as for bacon.

Kale: a cabbage with open curled green leaves. Used for making colcannon.

Legend: a traditional story which may or may not be true.

Leaven: the ferment which makes dough rise. This may be produced by the use of yeast, baking soda, bairm, buttermilk, or sour milk.

Lugh: one of the most important of the gods of Ireland. A sun god and a god of the arts and crafts; the father of Cúchulainn.

Myth: an ancient traditional story of gods or heroes; a commonly held belief that is purely fictional.

Porter: a weak, dark-colored beer, with a bitter flavor, which is brewed from charred or browned malt.

Potato Farls: Also known as potato cakes or fadge. Circles of potato bread cut into triangular pieces called farls.

St. Brigid: the Christian saint who is second only to St. Patrick. Her traditions have associations with those of the goddess Brigid, as does her feast day, which takes place on the same date.

Saltpeter: potassium nitrate, a white crystalline salty substance used both to preserve meat and to give it a rich pinky-red coloring.

Scallions: sometimes called spring onions. Both the white and green parts are used to flavor the milk which is used to make champ.

Scribe: an ancient or medieval official writer or copyist of manuscripts.

Soda Bread: made using brown, whole wheat, or refined white flour, raised by using baking soda with buttermilk. (see also Brown Soda; Soda Bread Flour)

Soda Bread Flour: a commercially prepared flour to which baking soda is added. (see also Brown Soda; Soda Bread; White Soda)

Soda Farls: triangular pieces of bread made from the basic soda bread mixture, rolled into a circle and cut into pieces known as farls. Sometimes referred to as "pointers."

Stout: extra strong porter.

Sweet Milk: milk from the cow.

Tír-na-nog: Tír is the Irish word for land or country—Tír na-nog—Land of Youth, Country of the Young. Here one gains eternal youth.

Tuatha de Danaan: the race that inhabited Ireland before the arrival of the Milesians (the ancestors of the Gaels). They were the gods of the pre-Christian Irish.

White Pudding: similar to black pudding, but not made with blood. White pudding contains oatmeal, lard, onion, herbs, and seasoning.

White Soda: soda bread made using refined white flour. (see also Brown Soda; Soda Bread; Soda Bread Flour)

index

Bibliography

Ronan Coghlan, Irish Myth and Legend, Appletree Press, Belfast 1985

Clare Connery, In an Irish Country Kitchen, Weidenfeld & Nicholson, London 1996

Kevin Danaher, The Year in Ireland, Mercier Press, Cork & Dublin 1972

Frank Delaney, The Celts, Harper Collins, London 1993. Legends of the Celts, Harper Collins, London 1994

Peter Berresford Ellis, A Dictionary of Irish Mythology, Oxford University Press, Oxford 1992

Evans, E. Estyn, Irish Folk Ways, Routledge & Kegan Paul Ltd, London 1957

Henry Glassie, Irish Folk History, O'Brien Press, Dublin 1982

Maire MacNeill, The Festival of Lughnasa, Oxford University Press, Oxford 1962

W. B. Yeats, The Book of Fairy and Folk Tales of Ireland, Smithmark, New York, 1996

Quotations

F. Delaney, Legends of the Celts p. 7

W. B. Yeats, The Book of Fairy and Folk Tales of Ireland p. 8

W. B. Yeats, "The Stolen Child," The Collected Poems of W. B. Yeats p. 9

Permission from A.P. Watt Ltd on behalf of Anne and Michael Yeats

Jonathan Swift, "Onions" pages 14, 30 & 73, "The Progress of Poetry" p. 90

Anonymous traditional rhyme, "Colcannon" pages 24, 46, 63, & 102

Anonymous traditional rhyme, "Champ" pages 100 & 101

Anonymous traditional rhyme, "Boxty" pages 115 & 130